Cover Image: Mick Brownfield

Illustrators

The Book Palace
Jubilee House
Bedwardine Road
Crystal Palace
London SE19 3AP

Email: IQ@bookpalace.com
Web: www.bookpalace.com
Contact GW: gw@bookpalace.com
Tel: 020 8768 0022
(From overseas +44 20 8768 0022)
Publisher: Geoff West
Editor & Art Director: Peter Richardson
Associate Editor & Designer: Bryn Havord
Consultant Editor: David Ashford
Featured Writers: Bryn Havord, David Ashford
and Peter Richardson
Website: Paul Tanner
Subscriptions & Distribution: David Howarth
Advertising: ads@bookpalace.com
illustratorsquarterly.com

illustrators ISBN 978-1-907081-12-5
ISSN 2052-6520
Issue Number Five Published Autumn 2013
Copyright © 2013 by The Book Palace Ltd.

illustrators is published quarterly.
Subscriptions for four issues:
£55 post free UK
£77 airmail Europe
£89 airmail USA/Rest of world

Available in the USA from **budplant.com**
Trade Orders: IQ@bookpalace.com
magazines@centralbooks.com

Printed in China by Prolong Press Ltd

ISSUE FIVE

CONTENTS

EDITORIAL

THIS ISSUE OF *illustrators* kicks off with an interview with Mick Brownfield as he looks back on a long and successful career which continues to this day. Mick is an artist whose lifelong obsession with illustration has not only made him a master of his medium but has underscored his art with a never ending series of slyly entertaining reference points which imbue his illustrations with a resonance that goes far beyond the mere fulfilment of an art director's brief.

The work of Brian Sanders has recently been brought to the fore again since he was asked to provide the artwork for the *Mad Men* Season Six poster, using the same technique that first brought his work to the attention of UK and US art directors in the 1960s. Sanders' career and art have now spanned over five decades, and as Bryn Havord's text reveals, there is much more to Sanders then has been revealed in the recent media coverage this commission spawned.

Janet and Anne Grahame Johnstone's illustrations were everywhere for much of the latter part of the last century. Their work was as familiar to children and their parents as the illustrations of Mabel Lucy Atwell and Kate Greenaway had been to previous generations, but the story of how these twin sisters achieved their enchanting art is less familiar and we are therefore delighted to have the opportunity to share with their story with you.

Derek Eyles may have been a little laid back in comparison to many of his contemporaries, but when it came to creating dynamic and action packed artwork designed to thrill his schoolboy readership, he was in a league of his own. David Ashford reveals much more about the man whose art was often used as a guide by editors to show "how it should be done", especially when depicting horses.

Finally, with *Book Palace*'s eagerly anticpated *Frank Bellamy's Heros the Spartan*, Bryn Havord castes his eyes over its pages and recalls his days working at the offices of *Eagle* comics.

The opinions expressed in *illustrators* are those of the writers, and are not necessarily those of the editor and publishers. The accuracy of the authentication of all images is the responsibility of the contributors.

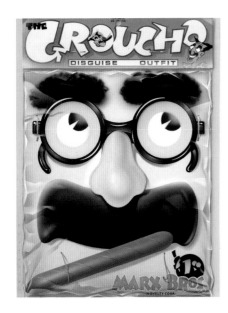

Mick Brownfield

ABOVE: Groucho Disguise Outfit for Portal Publications. 1980.
ABOVE RIGHT: W. C. Fields for Portal publications 1980.
FACING PAGE: 'Call Centre' illustration for *Reader's Digest* magazine.

Peter Richardson talks to one of the UK's most successful and consistently inventive illustrators about his career and the insecurities that drive his creativity.

PR. Looking back, would you say that you always wanted to be an illustrator?
MB. I did but I wasn't quite sure what it was. I had a distant relative who was a commercial artist. I wasn't really aware of the mechanics of what was going on but he could draw really well. He could draw Red Indians. I'd heard the words in films as well—commercial art. I wanted to draw but I knew I wouldn't make a living as a painter or whatever. It was something that was always in the back of my mind. I always felt the urge towards the commercial subjects.
PR. When you were growing up did you have heroes in illustration and comic

ABOVE TOP: The five year old Mick Brownfield and the artist as he is today with his dog, the legendary Chipp.
ABOVE: Painting by Brownfield when he was 12 inspired by an illustration from *Look and Learn*.
FACING PAGE: Page from sketchbook.

books that you thought; "Hey! This is it, this is what I really want to do?

MB. Yes, but I didn't know what their names were, except of course for Denis McLoughlin in the *Buffalo Bill Annual*. He was the most obvious. The most visible. I can remember responding to the drawings. I would enjoy a comic or a book more if the illustrations were strong—so yes.

PR. I remember you telling me in an earlier conversation that you used to cut out the Buffalo Bill pictures and stick them on the wall.

MB. Yes they were wonderful I always responded very much to film. I was a huge film fan. I responded particularly to the beginning of a film, the way the image and the titles would make a wonderful whole. Lettering and type—I'm sure that's where that comes from. I wasn't really aware of it as illustration as such, it was more a part of my life.

PR. So it was more of a subconscious yearning?

MB. Yes, well I always drew, but I tended to do comic strips based on a film I had seen. I'd always add the title of the film in some strong way. But films and comics did seem to have an enormous influence on me and that's why in the sixth form, particularly when I first went to art school, I was puzzled by the subject matter I was encouraged to draw, which was still-life, industrial landscapes, whatever was considered to be worthy in the sixties. When Pop Art started you realised you could respond to popular subject matter without it having to be disguised. That was a big breakthrough for me, seeing the work of Peter Blake and thinking that's where I want to be.

PR. When you first went to art college was there a local college?

MB. Yes, I went to Walthamstow and then I went to Hornsey for three years, leaving in '69.

PR. Was that the end of your art college years?

MB. Yes, I wasn't encouraged to go any further. I wasn't a particularly good student, I had a very bad attendance record. Mainly because I enjoyed

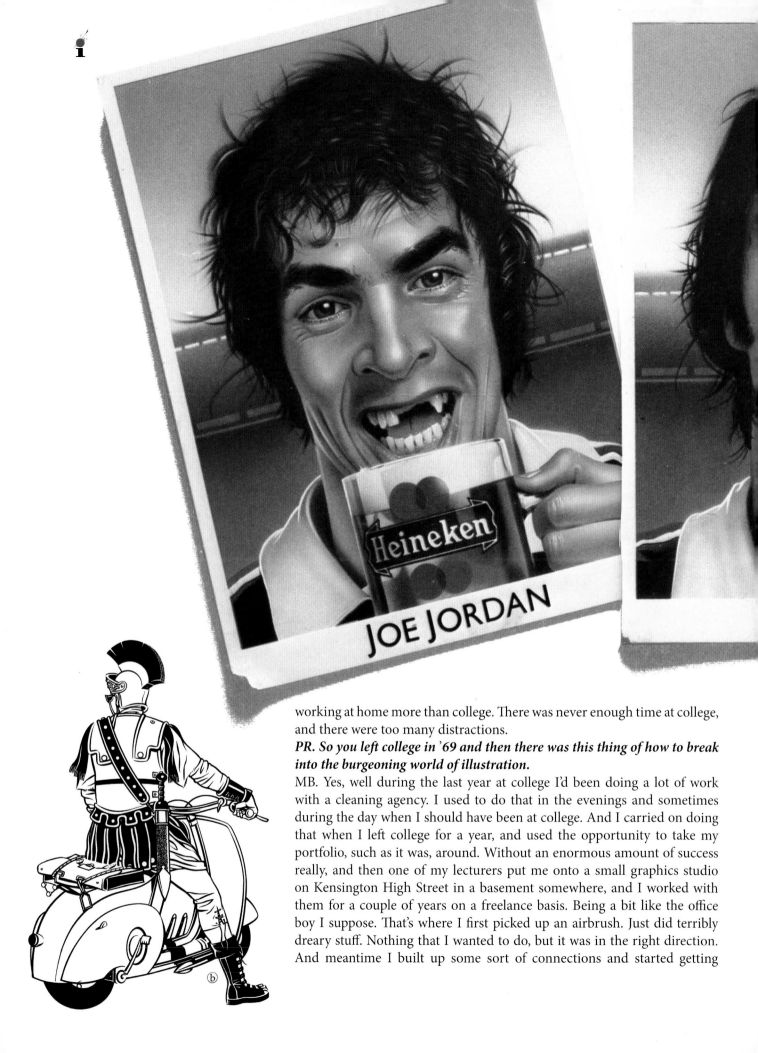

JOE JORDAN

working at home more than college. There was never enough time at college, and there were too many distractions.

PR. So you left college in '69 and then there was this thing of how to break into the burgeoning world of illustration.

MB. Yes, well during the last year at college I'd been doing a lot of work with a cleaning agency. I used to do that in the evenings and sometimes during the day when I should have been at college. And I carried on doing that when I left college for a year, and used the opportunity to take my portfolio, such as it was, around. Without an enormous amount of success really, and then one of my lecturers put me onto a small graphics studio on Kensington High Street in a basement somewhere, and I worked with them for a couple of years on a freelance basis. Being a bit like the office boy I suppose. That's where I first picked up an airbrush. Just did terribly dreary stuff. Nothing that I wanted to do, but it was in the right direction. And meantime I built up some sort of connections and started getting

some work. As I was being paid something like £15.00 a week it wasn't hard to make more than that, and so I left there and that was when I became a proper freelance illustrator, which was in 1973. I think when I left there I was making £35.00 a week and then the first week I went freelance I made a £100.00.

So I thought, "What the Hell have I been doing?" I was cautious, because my father was always an employed person and had been very nervous about money, and it had rubbed off on me. I was recently married and had a child on the way, and hadn't been able to save and was a bit uncertain. And really it was gravy from then on.

PR. So, your career really took off from 1973 onwards. It was a fairly propitious era for illustration.

MB. It was, yes—tremendously so. I started the same time as a lot of other people, who are all well known and still working.

PR. So did you do it all by networking, rather than promotion?

FACING PAGE: 'Quo Vadis Baby', the artist as Roman warrior complete with folio strapped to his trusty Vespa.
ABOVE: Joe Jordan poster for Heineken beer campaign 1978. Art directed by Tony Kaye for Collet, Dickinson and Pearce, a series of 48 sheet posters were devised to illustrate the line "Heineken refreshes the parts other beers cannot reach".

7

The magazine that tells you what's on and where to go in London.
August 31-September 6 1979
No.489 35p

Time Out

Sci-Fi with a human face.

Twenty-one years after the exploits of Professor Quatermass last jangled the airwaves, the old prophet returns in a story of civilisation's declining years. We ask author Nigel Kneale how he kept psychological Sci-Fi alive in the age of 'The Alien.'

ABOVE: A beautifully perverse depiction of 'Prince' for *The Sunday Times Magazine.*
ABOVE RIGHT AND FACING PAGE: Two consecutive weeks of Brownfield *Time Out* covers enabled the artist to pull off one of his most impressive coups, when he depicted Ridley Scott's newly released 'Alien' bursting through the previous week's 'Quatermass' cover.

MB. Yes I did. I got an agent the same year—1973. I was recommended to an agent called Wendy Booth, in Garrick Street and there was a studio there where Ian Beck was working, Glyn Boyde Hart and a couple of other people. So I joined up with them although I never actually worked there. So I stayed with those guys up until the Jenni Stone period.

PR. So that period takes you through the seventies. It was you building up a reputation.

MB. Well I think I built it up very quickly. I was being asked to lecture and teach within a couple of years of going freelance. I've always been very lucky in getting quite high profile jobs to do, always done lots of magazines and covers and work that people see. Other people have careers—quite splendid careers doing work that never sees the light of day. Whereas I've done hundreds of *Time Out* covers and I've always liked that, I've always loved to have the most covers out that week. I've always been terribly competitive in that way.

PR. I remember one **Time Out** *cover you did, because you were doing so many of them you did them several weeks running, when the film 'Alien'*

Text continues on page 12

The magazine that tells you what's on and where to go in London.
September 7-13 1979
No.490 35p

Time Out

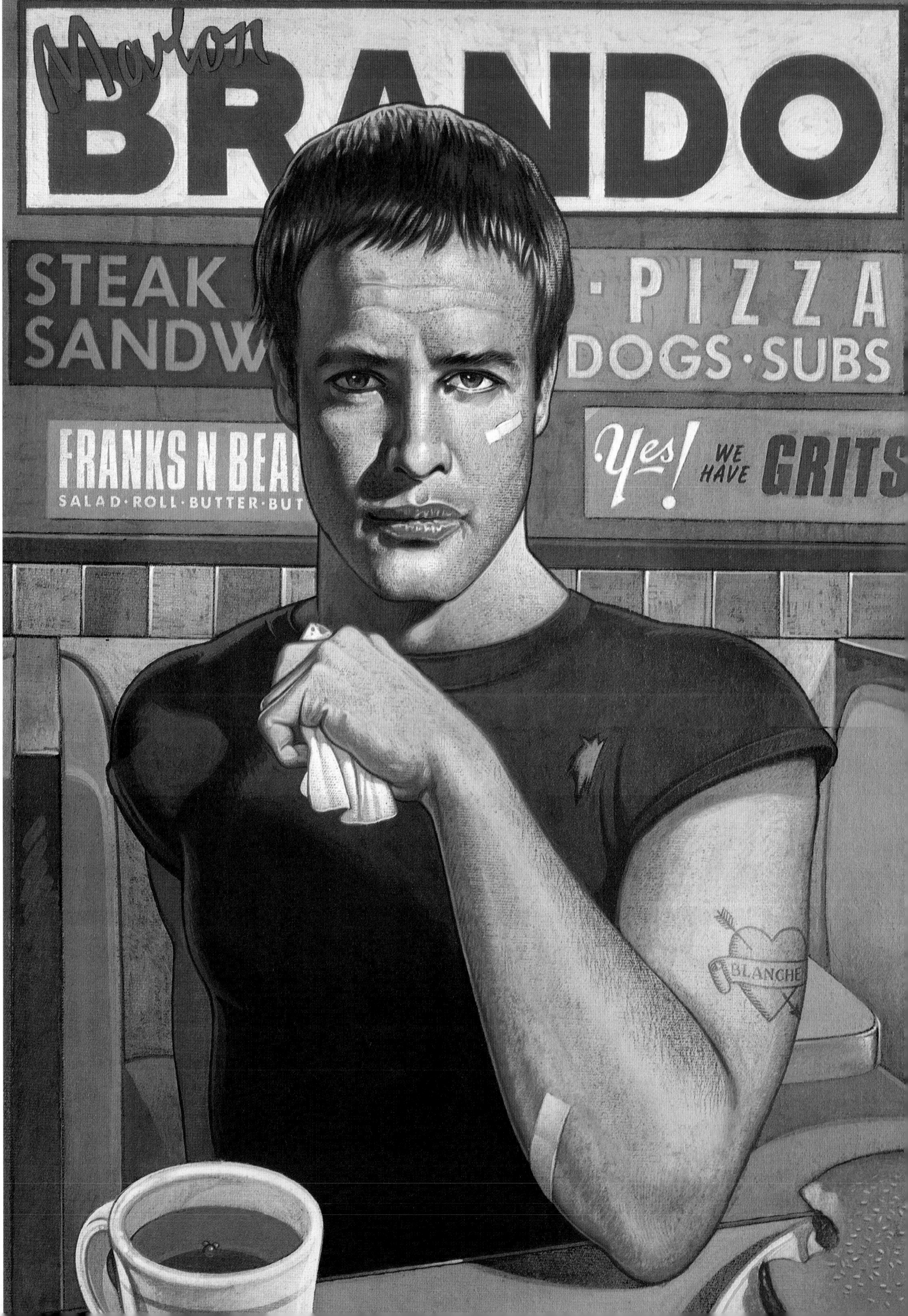
Marlon
BRANDO
STEAK
SANDW
PIZZA
DOGS · SUBS
FRANKS N BEA
SALAD · ROLL · BUTTER · BUT
Yes! WE HAVE GRITS
BLANCHE

JOHN WAYNE

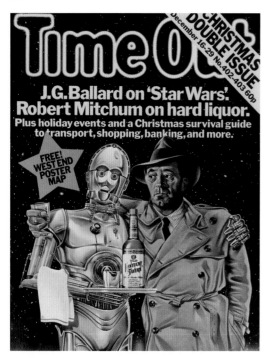

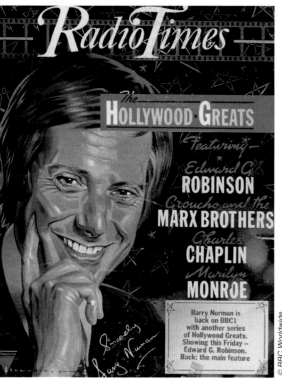

ABOVE AND TOP: Two *Time Out* covers from 1977 and a *Radio Times* cover from 1979 were typical of the high profile work that Brownfield was able to attract from the outset of his career.

Text continued from page 8

came out you had the alien bursting through the previous week's cover.

MB. Yes, of course it was primitive technology then. Nowadays you'd just have to provide two drawings in a computer. Then you actually had to fake it up and then shoot it.

PR. And that was in the day—well you still do it—of doing fairly complex masking and soft masking with an airbrush.

MB. Yes, it was also a time of very late nights and working all night. Then it was exciting and thrilling and thinking, "Oh this is what real illustrators do". But I wouldn't dream of doing it now. It would kill me to do it now. But the more work I did—one of the advantages of being freelance the busier you are the better it is for you. You get all the money. I'm always astonished when people tell me they're terribly busy and they tell me what they're doing and to me its nothing. They've got six months to do it and I'd do it in a working week.

PR. Presumably you're one of these illustrators who function best if they've got a lot of work on.

MB. Yes. Its very good for me mentally, I'm very neurotic, I'm constantly being told—needlessly. And the busier I am the more the demons are shut out really. Because you've got to think about what you are doing, rather than what you're not doing. Its just one of those things I have to live with.

PR. Well, bearing that in mind, have you, over the last forty years, found it easy to maintain a consistent flow of work?

MB. Totally! Yes always. Which is extraordinary. Because I do so many different things there was always something to do. You might be in the middle of a big advertising job, a poster or something and somebody might say do you want to do a cover for *The Sunday Times Magazine*. Do you work harder, or do you say, "No I can't do it" and concentrate on the one job you've got? I can't be like that, I can't pass up on anything.

PR. Working in all these different areas gives you great opportunity to pay homage to all sorts of different illustrators.

MB. (Laughs) Other illustrators might not call it homage. Yes, for instance yesterday I got a call out of the blue from a costume designer, she's working on a Pepsi commercial. I don't know if you've seen the one with Beckham and he's a cowboy. Well this is a gladiator thing, so in a morning I had to design four or five costumes based on very, very poor sketches by her and really make them work. I love doing that. I really enjoy that. It was all over by two o'clock. And I'd earned my day's money—a very good day's money. And everybody was amazed and thrilled by that. Its that old thing of, "Look at me Mum I'm riding a bike with no hands". A lot of that in it too…

PR. Oh yes, I think so because its one of those jobs that people just shake their heads and can't see it as a viable way of making a living. Presumably your approach is a constant way of proving that you're succeeding.

MB. Yes… I guess it is and when you're quiet or you've got problems, and you're as weak minded as I am, you immediately think its because I'm no longer any good and you forget about that completely. You should forget about that immediately and concentrate on what you should be doing, which is the work. I've often thought about going to see a psychiatrist to see if he could explain why something which so obviously isn't true should be such a problem to me.

PR. I think these feelings of unease are fairly germane to a lot of illustrators at the moment, do you have any ideas as to why?

MB. Well in the previous recession in the early nineties I had tremendously good years. It didn't affect me in any way at all. I just think that in some ways its my turn and things are so different now that if more magazines get canned, there's less money in advertising, spending on different things. I really think that the glory days, certainly for me are over. I'm still doing lots of work but I look at it differently now. I don't really have anything to prove, I'm not going to be more successful than I was or make more money

CHEESE

ABOVE TOP LEFT: 'Lips' for *Marie Claire* magazine, France.
ABOVE RIGHT: 'Bogus' a double page spread illustration in the style of pin-up artist Alberto Vargas for *The Tatler* magazine.
ABOVE: 'Cheese', illustration for *Company* magazine 1982.

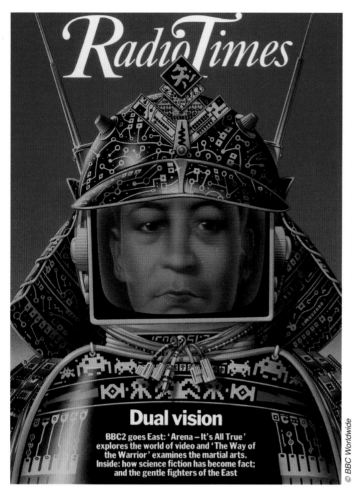

BEST FOR TV | BEST FOR RADIO | BEST FOR FILMS LONDON

www.radiotimes.com 9

RadioTimes

14–20 AUGUST 2004

MOVIES TO CHANGE YOUR LIFE

RT's top 50 films of all time – with a difference. See p14

EXCLUSIVE: DAY-BY-DAY OLYMPICS TV GUIDE
Eight-page pull-out special – including full interactive listings

ABOVE TOP AND FACING PAGE: Although famed for his Christmas covers, Mick Brownfield's inventive and punchy work has hosted a variety of *Radio Times* themes throughout his career.
ABOVE: 'Maigret'—an editorial illustration for *Radio Times*.

than I have done. But I've been doing it for over forty years and I think that's something to be proud off and not worry about really. I mean obviously when you have to live and this is how I make my living, there's nothing else I can do. I'm certainly much too old to think about anything else… no need to. I still have to make a living and I want to go on a bit longer. I pretty much do take all the jobs that I'm offered, because they're always nice. Top of the range—big newspapers, big agencies, big publishers or whatever. People sometimes phone up from *Yellow Pages*, I remember one said, "would you come and do some cartoons at our barbecue?"

PR. (Laughs)

MB. And you know I did think about it. (laughs) I mean that is what I'm supposed to be doing isn't it? The good thing is that I've always managed to work for top clients. I mean there's a lot of below the line work for magazines and advertising. There's certainly not as much… I mean I'm never going to be doing any more Heineken posters. But you feel pretty good when you get that kind of work that is liked so much that its going to get in the D&AD book (Design and Art Directors Annual) and getting a silver medal that makes a big difference, I felt. But particularly with advertising, I'm well known in advertising, I'm known to be useful and quick. Which is a good thing to be, not necessarily in one style but someone who can turn stuff around quickly, that they've got a problem with or don't know quite who to use. I tend to get that kind of work.

PR. Yes and largely through reputation rather than a lot of promotion.

Text continues on page 18

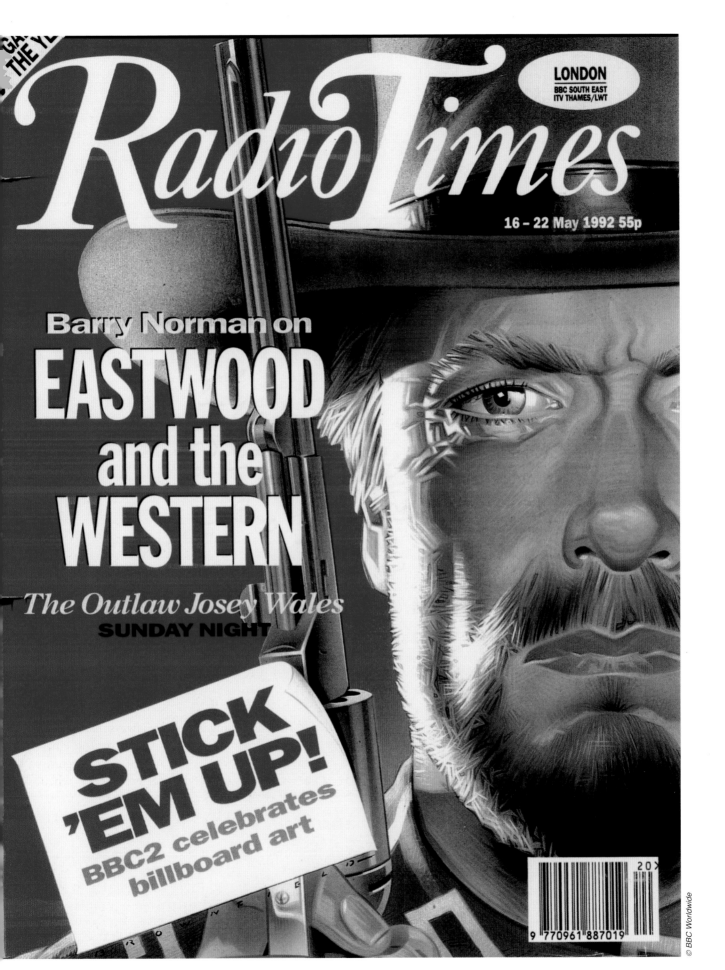

15

ABOVE TOP: Brownfield holds the record for illustrating the most *Radio Times* Christmas covers. From the left, covers for the 1992, 1995, 1996 and 1998 *Radio Times*.
ABOVE: Christmas stamp proposal for the Royal Mail.
RIGHT: Cover for the Christmas edition of *TV Times*.
FAR RIGHT: *Radio Times* Christmas cover for 2009.
FACING PAGE BOTTOM: Rough and finished artwork for the Christmas 2012 *TV and Satellite Weekly*.

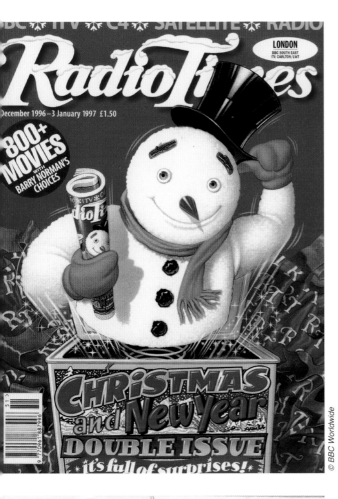

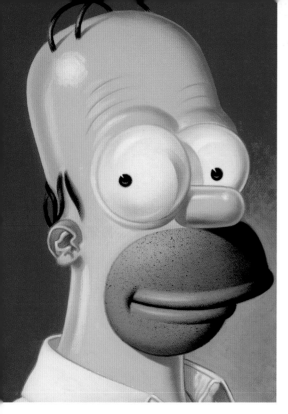

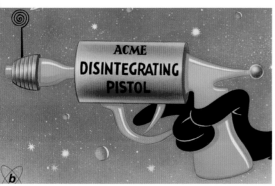

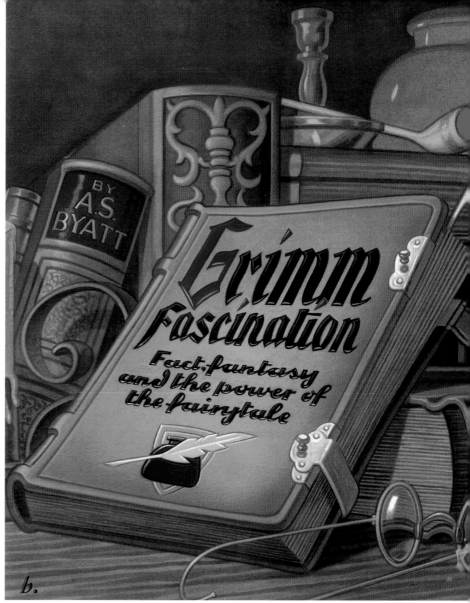

ABOVE TOP: 'Homer'; 2D TV icon is given added depth in one of Brownfield's personal paintings.
ABOVE: 'Ray Gun', another self-initiated painting pays homage to animator Tex Avery and Maurice Noble, whose background paintings added extra lustre to many a Disney and Warner Bros cartoon.
ABOVE RIGHT: A cover for *The Guardian* Christmas book review, tips a hat in the direction of another legendary Disney animation background artist—Claude Coats.
FACING PAGE: Illustration of an alien cinema cashier for *The Sunday Times* culture section.

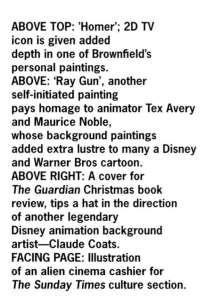

Text continued from page 14

MB. Yes, I've never done any of that. Certainly not since I've been freelance, I'd been completely without an agent only since 1993, I'm now currently repped by C.I.A. (Central Illustration Agency).

PR. Do you feel that you could have done the work without the agent?

MB. Yuh I do, totally yeah. Absolutely, but as I say, I felt everybody else had an agent, so I should have one too. When I didn't have an agent I was even prouder of the fact I was doing so well. Without one it was brilliant.

PR. Some illustrators do feel much more secure with an agent, not just because they're going to generate more work, but because they're going to negotiate better fees.

MB. I don't believe in any of that. It was only until a few years ago when I could see that things were certainly getting more difficult that I felt it might be useful to have one. But I'm very happy to do all the stuff that agents do. My wife looks after a lot of that, but I like all that, dealing with clients direct, asking for ridiculous fees. That's the side of things that I like—I'm a very commercial animal.

PR. Would you say that fees have kept in line with inflation?

MB. All those things, they haven't kept in line with inflation, in most cases

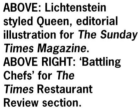

ABOVE: Lichtenstein styled Queen, editorial illustration for *The Sunday Times Magazine*.
ABOVE RIGHT: 'Battling Chefs' for *The Times* Restaurant Review section.

in my experience they've gone down. Money was worth more thirty years ago and in some cases the fees were higher then they are now, certainly in editorial. And in advertising, its hard to get those fees. I find it hard to get them. I've got a little table of fees in my head and I've had to adjust that. People kind of laugh when I mention that.

PR. Yes, because whenever I meet other illustrators and this subject comes up, we all agree that we're earning what we were thirty years ago—if we're lucky! Have you any thoughts on this?

MB. I presume because there's an economic downturn they've got less money to spend but there again maybe art buyers are tougher. In the halcyon days an agency would just pass the mark-up onto their client, the fee wouldn't even come into consideration they were spending so much money on everything else that was just another of the expenses. Now they will always try to knock you down, for no reason, even if its a reasonable fee that you're quoting, they'll still feel they have to talk you down. Obviously there are still times when I get very well paid for doing something that's not that difficult, but I seem to spend more time doing more difficult jobs for less money, which I find highly frustrating and annoying. You know you've got a whole load of work to do and if its not well paid then that's really annoying.

PR. Would you say that there is a lack of appreciation of illustration?

MB. Yes—totally. Certainly in this country, I wouldn't say that was true in other

Text continues on page 26

Graham Coton (1926 – 2003)

Oil on Canvas. Original painting 1990
The Memphis Belle B-17 Bomber in 1943 (1000mm x 760mm)

This is one many paintings by Graham Coton now available to purchase.
We also have a large selection of other military paintings by artists such as
Fortunino Matania, Giorgio De Gasapri, Jordi Penalva, Alessandro Biffignandi, Cecil Doughty,
Patrick Nicolle, Ron Embleton, Wilf Hardy, Nino Caroselli, Angus McBride and many more.
Why not visit us online now?

Graham Coton (1926 – 2003)

Acrylic on board. Original cover art to War Picture Library #880
(September 1973) "The Dark Terror" (450mm x 600mm)

ILLUSTRATION ART GALLERY

The world's largest selection of original illustration art
www.iartg.com   Tel: 020 8768 0022 (from outside UK+44 20 8768 0022)

Over 5000 original paintings and drawings by over 600 artists

Graham Coton (1926 - 2003)

Acrylic on board. Original cover art to Battle Picture Library #428
(November 1969) "Tank Alert" (320mm x 420mm)

ILLUSTRATION ART GALLERY

The world's largest selection of original illustration art
www.iartg.com   Tel: 020 8768 0022 (from outside UK+44 20 8768 0022)

Over 5000 original paintings and drawings by over 600 artists

Graham Coton (1926 – 2003)

Acrylic on board. Original painting 1975
"Big Boy" X4018 Locomotive Union Pacific Railroad (500mm x 600mm)

ILLUSTRATION ART GALLERY

The world's largest selection of original illustration art
www.iartg.com Tel: 020 8768 0022 (from outside UK+44 20 8768 0022)

Over 5000 original paintings and drawings by over 600 artists

IN THE NEXT ISSUE

*We draw back
the curtain on the work
of one of the
20th century's premier
romantic painters
in an in-depth
feature devoted to
the life and
career of
Walter Wyles.*

**Plus the adrenalised art of Graham Coton, the sublimely satirical Dave
Gaskill, and the art of the travel poster with Laurence Fish.**

Text continued from page 20

ABOVE TOP: 'Coffee Break AD 1960'.
Kirk Douglas on the set of 'Spartacus'
from an ongoing homage to Hollywood's
"Sword and Sandals" epics.
ABOVE: Sci-Fi themed cover for *The*
Guardian **Life section**
FACING PAGE: 'Quatermass', a self
promotional illustration featuring TV
writer Nigel Kneale.

places, particularly like America. I don't think its ever been in this country. I've never felt that to be the case here. It seems to be regarded as a cheaper way to fill a gap. I don't know why it is like that in this country, obviously individual art directors can be very appreciative and knowledgeable. But in general I don't get the feeling that its regarded as a cut above marquetry. But then again I've never really got used to the fact that people are asking me to do illustrations for money. I still think its an amazing thing to be asked to do. I think its important to remember that and not get too prima-donna'ish. Because its swings and roundabouts, you might get a lousy job that's badly paid, but they might come up with a wonderful job that's fantastically well paid. You've got to try and be helpful. I'm very aware of the importance of not being too difficult. I mean there are difficult people.
PR. It can be a huge impediment, you can be brilliant but if you're difficult
you're destined for disappointment.
MB. I'm actually doing some book jackets, I'm drawing the roughs as we're speaking that somebody else started, but the client couldn't work with him. He just found his attitude too aggressive, he wasn't able to accept anybody

PICTURE
MONDAY
4MARCH 1957
GEL KNEALE
TV's
cket Man
QUATERMASS II
4D QUATERMASS!
www.mickbrownfield.com

ABOVE: Illustration for the *Radio Times*.
BELOW: 'Art Monster', a typically feisty and in your face T-shirt design created in 2004.
FACING PAGE: Self promotional card depicting well known *Mad* icon Alfred E Neuman as a beatnik artist.

else's ideas. He was very good but the client just wasn't enjoying the relationship and so he went somewhere else. It seems to me to be common sense—be nice to the person who's paying you, even if you can't stand the guy and he's a complete idiot, keep that to yourself. I can't think of any occasion that I've lost it and shouted at somebody. Certainly I may have slammed the phone down but I really can't think of any occasion…

PR. Yes, its very counterproductive.

MB. I haven't even raised my voice. I've wanted to, believe me. I think that one of the worst parts of the job these days is that you are dealing with a generation of people that aren't visually literate. They don't know the history of illustration or have any particular affection for it. Pretty much everybody I work for is half my age. And they're all terribly nice to me, but they don't seem particularly educated, they can't express themselves at all well. When you go in to a meeting and its a young team they can't talk, they just sit there and grunt occasionally. I find myself completely running the show saying we need to do this and that and whatever and they don't have any way of communicating. I find that very difficult because over the years I've worked with some wonderful people, really intelligent, amusing people I'm very fond of. But they're retiring, or working in commercials or just not in the business any more, and I miss them.

PR. There was a golden age of illustration of really highly trained art directors and art editors who loved illustration and knew the history of it.

MB. Well yes, when I was in my twenties I was working with people who were forty or fifty, so they'd come from the very early days, certainly as we know it. People like David Hillman at Pentagram, the big names, they're just not there.

PR. I gather that you still work entirely traditionally…
MB. Yes—I do.

PR. None of this cheating with Photoshop.
MB. Well, I've got all those things. I've never really had the time to sit down and learn how to do all those things. I mean my friend Paul Slater, who also works traditionally, he does use a surprising amount of computer work, even though it never can be detected. He's offered to teach me how to do it. But I'm kind of technophobic. I haven't necessarily seen anything, certainly in the way that I work that I could do better by doing it on the computer. If you're doing stuff that is obviously computer driven and looks like it—and I know what it can do, and its great, but I don't particularly feel that I need it. We do obviously need it to send artwork and its an incredibly useful tool in that way. Its that classic thing of they put a shadow under something and it never works for me, it always looks like a computer shadow. Its not organic. Its purely my opinion and I know there's some great stuff done on computers here and in America, without it there wouldn't be *Toy Story* and that sort of stuff and that's magnificent. To me they might as well be using magic, because I've no idea how its done, I think its unbelievable. But its no better than *Pinocchio*. I've just been looking through one of those big (Disney) books, 'The Art Of…' or whatever, looking for a nice sunset and some of the backgrounds, which is what I'm most interested in rather than the animation, are so beautiful. Watercoloury backgrounds of Geppeto's workshop and that sort of thing are so fantastic… just drool-making. To think they did that under enormous pressure and without any real consideration of anything "art", it was just an incidental thing in the background. I think the computer has been responsible for an awful lot of downgrading of illustration. Like

FACING PAGE: Full page
illustration for *Ultratravel Quarterly*
ABOVE: Harvey Keitel
in 'Reservoir Dogs' for
Sight and Sound.
BELOW: Illustration for *WPP Journal*.

ABOVE AND FACING PAGE:
The golden age of travel
posters is revisited
in these P&O press ads
that Brownfield
created in 1990.

for instance I'm looking through my *Guardian* this morning—I do quite a lot of work for *The Guardian*, there's lots of illustrations in there and they're almost all computer generated. Because obviously they're pretty quick and in most cases seem to me to be just a photograph that's put in and doctored up and a couple of squiggles and that's pretty much it, which is OK—do it once. But what are those guys going to do next? You know. And they're all leaving college with this generic style and I don't see where its going to go. It can't develop particularly, unless they're better artists—the computer hides a multitude of sins, I would imagine. I have people from magazines phoning saying, "we're all standing around your artwork" and the younger ones say, "we can't believe its not printed", they've never seen flat artwork: ever. And that's nice but it makes me feel incredibly weird.

PR. But you still send your artwork out as flat artwork?

MB. Well I've only got an A4 scanner, I live in London so its no problem for me to pick up things up or my wife delivers them. But in general more and more stuff for magazines is being sent by computer. We couldn't operate without a computer, nobody can, but I still don't feel an enormous urge to use it, because I enjoy... I'm covered in black dust at the moment from

Text continues on page 38

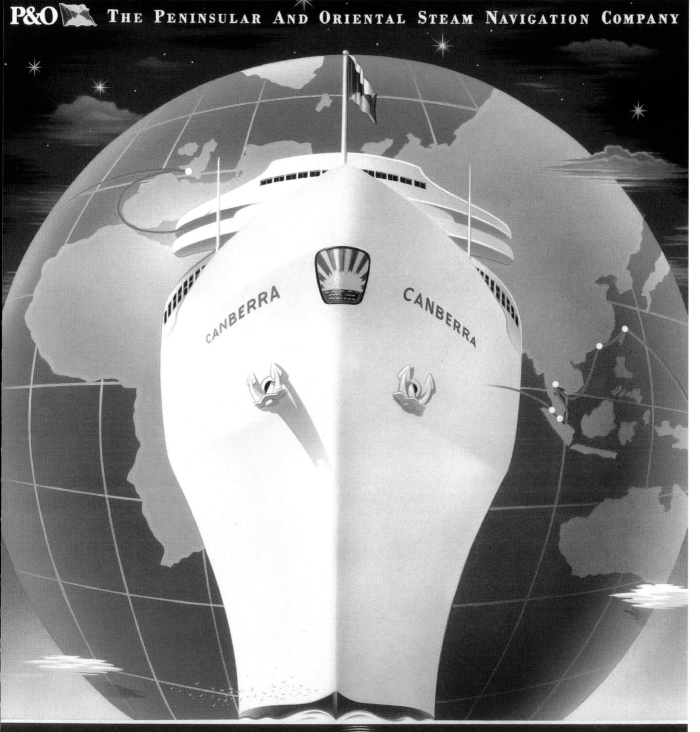

SOUTHAMPTON TO SOUTHAMPTON
VIA
THE WORLD

On Monday 8th January 1990
CANBERRA
sails westwards round the globe via such
EXOTIC DESTINATIONS
AS BERMUDA, SAN FRANCISCO, FIJI, SYDNEY, HONG KONG AND BOMBAY
returning 90 days later.

CANBERRA

PLEASE SEND ME A COPY OF THE 1990 WORLD CRUISE BROCHURE

Name _____

Address _____

Post to: Canberra World Cruises, Harrington Dock, Liverpool X, L70 1AX.

WORLD CRUISE 1990

Fares from **£4,680** *per person.*
SHORTER PASSAGES ALSO AVAILABLE FROM 12 TO 71 DAYS IN LENGTH.

BOOK THROUGH
any ABTA travel agent or telephone Reservations on 01-836 9881. Send for our lavish FULL COLOUR brochure.

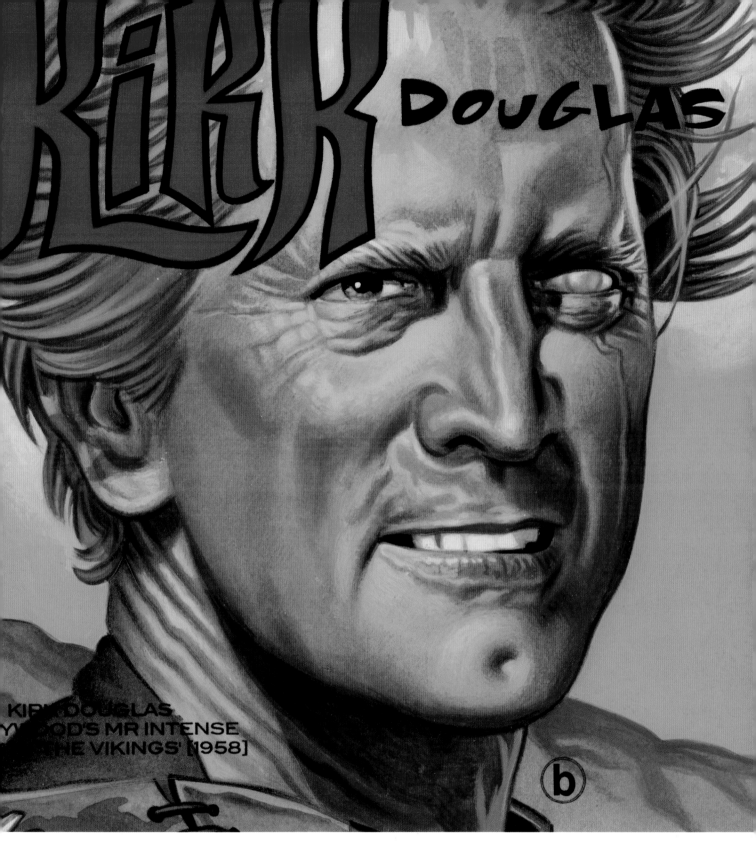

KiRK DOUGLAS

KIRK DOUGLAS
...WOOD'S MR INTENSE
...THE VIKINGS' [1958]

ⓑ

FACING PAGE: 'Pepium'. Full
page illustration for *Premiere* magazine
with portrait of Hollywood
'Sword and Sandals'
heart-throb Steve Reeves.
ABOVE: Portrait of Kirk Douglas
from 'The Vikings' 1958.

ABOVE: Poster artwork
featuring *Tony the Tiger* for
Kellogs. Commissioned by
Leo Burnett 2009.
RIGHT: *Coca Cola*
trademark.
FACING PAGE: *Coca Cola*
poster for Publicis in Paris...
note the extra finger! The
artist spotted the error
and the final version
appeared with the regulation
number of digits.

Text continued from page 32

ABOVE: One of a series of fashion illustrations for *Commons & Sense* magazine Tokyo. A sheet of tracing paper was laid over the background collage to create an opaque effect.
ABOVE RIGHT: 'Holperstolper' Poster art for a German company.

pencil and I like that. I like painting, and later on I'll be doing a drawing for *The Daily Telegraph* which I'm doing in nice watercolour washes and fluffy pink clouds and I shall really enjoy it. I'm really looking forward to it. I enjoy drawing and painting. When I'm not busy I still feel compelled to do it. And more and more of these things I do on canvas, because to me that means its a proper painting. Its fun—its lovely fun!

PR. But when you look at the illustration industry, what advice would you give to a young person wanting to enter this tortured profession?

MB. I'd do it.

PR. You'd do it?

MB. Yes in real terms I would imagine there's an enormous amount of work out there. You know we've more than had that, "You're never going to do a double spread in *The Sunday Times Magazine* ever again". That might be true, but there's still an awful lot of illustration out there. I mean there are an awful lot more places to use it I would think. But I think to be an illustrator you've got to have a ticking temperament. And apart from the neuroses of worrying about money, I think I have that. You've got to have endless patience, endless time to put into things if I can. If I've got a job that suddenly I've got two or three days, it might even be a small *Radio Times* job, I will take that time and do something extra special. Because firstly its got that special wow

factor—I'm not saying that it would be a better drawing then one I had to do in an afternoon, but sometimes its good to take the time and consider things and think, "Well there's another approach I can take, let's try this." Which is completely impossible normally in my job because there's never any time, its always on the spot and I respond to that. I like that journalistic approach to work. But in a way you're always thinking well what's the easiest way I can do this… I know I can do it in this style in the time, because you can't afford to suddenly realise its not working.

PR. Because you have to a certain extent paired down your technique ?
MB. Well yes—my favourite area to work in is newspapers and magazines. I can't really afford to indulge in some of the work you get asked to do—when people ask you to do a poster pastiche. I always think when people ask you to that, then its the most time consuming, difficult thing to do. A big lavish pastiche of a film poster and they've only got three hundred quid and they need it later on the same day. Now in that case you have to persuade them that maybe it would work with just one face, with just part of a face, with a dramatic close up, maybe in just one colour or two colours. All that sort of stuff. You can't do it. If it was an advertising job where you've got two weeks and they're going to pay four thousand quid—absolutely go for it! Push out the boat a bit! You've got to cut your cloth according to your means. I don't have rates for a job. There's some advertising work where you get a fortune for it, but that's not true necessarily of editorial. It depends

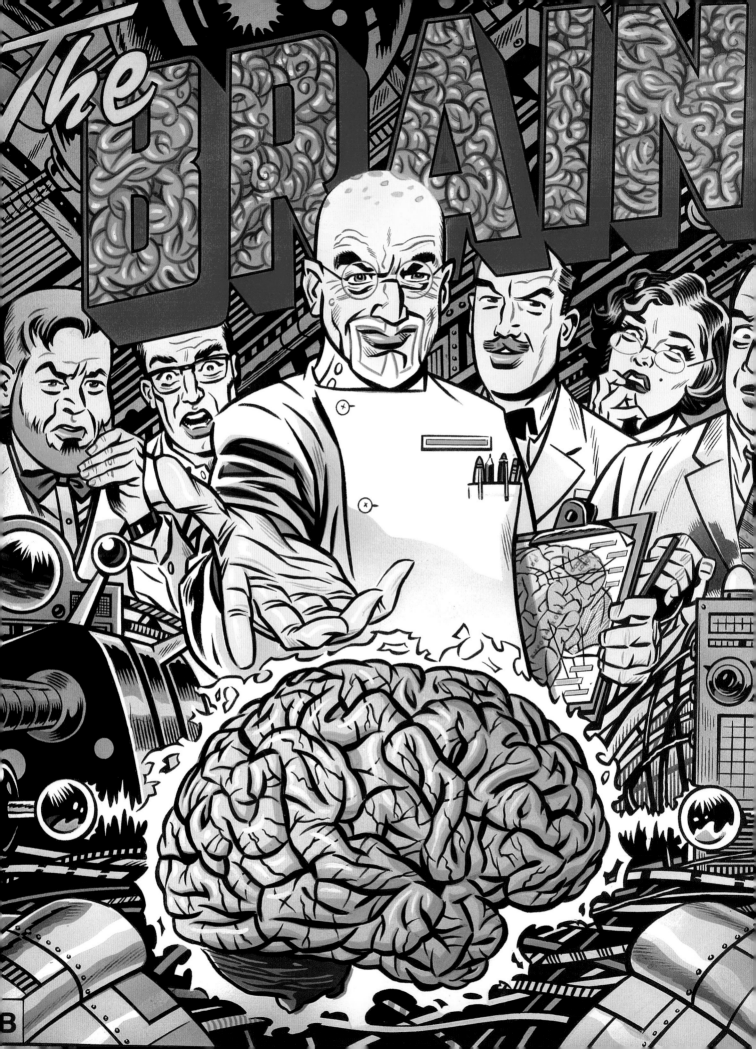

on how much you want to do the job, and the art director and what he wants—its about getting real about the thing. I'm just trying to do the best I can with every job I get. I'm never happy with what I do, I'm not a big fan of my work. I've got some things around, I've got lots and lots of framed paintings—my "greatest hits". They're not on the wall, they're lying against the wall. Because if you haven't seen a painting you've done for five years or so, you see it suddenly—the whole thing. After that you start to think, "Oh I wish I hadn't used that green, or why did I do that…" Totally difficult to be objective. That's why I always survive by getting work.

ts all the same person, the same job, if you're doing a Heineken poster, a cover for *The Sunday Times Magazine* and a film poster all in the same week, then that's got to make you feel pretty good—don't you think? ●

● *To see more of Mick Brownfield's work go to* **www.mickbrownfield.com**

FACING PAGE:'The Brain'
an illustration for *The Saturday Telegraph*, 2012.
ABOVE LEFT: Father's Day card for Dunhill.
ABOVE TOP: Full page illustration for *Admap*.
ABOVE: 'Cocktails' an editorial illustration for *Cargo* magazine New York.

ABOVE: The illustration by Brian Sanders which appeared in *Woman's Mirror* in 1965 showing the 'bubble and streak' technique which was achieved with Liquitex acrylic paints and mediums.

Brian Sanders

Bryn Havord looks at the work of the man whose art captured the look of the '60s, and inspired Mad Men's Matthew Weiner to commission the artist to depict those halcyon days for the launch of the show's sixth season.

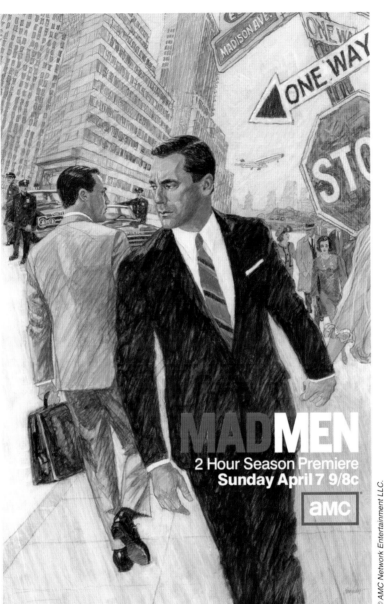

LEFT: The finished Mad Men painting created from a sketch made by Matthew Weiner, and a collection of photographic reference supplied by the programme makers to ensure period accuracy, depicting Don Draper, the show's lead character experiencing a 'doppelgänger' moment on a New York City sidewalk.

BRIAN SANDERS WAS A JUDOKA at The Budokwai in the west end of London, and I was a judoka at The Judokan in Hammersmith. Fortunately, we never met on a judo mat, but on the carpet in my office at *Woman's Mirror,* when I commissioned him to illustrate a ten-part romantic serial for the magazine. It was in the mid 1960s, and Sanders was part of a new breed of upcoming illustrators, who worked out of a studio at Artist Partners; an agency which was run on the lines of the famous Charles E. Cooper Studios in New York City.

If we'd had a crystal ball, we could have looked forward to the end of 2012. Matthew Weiner, the creator of *Mad Men,* the celebrated television series, set in the art-directed world of 1960s American advertising, decided to market the sixth series in the style of a 1960s ad man,

and remembering the painterly illustrations used on Trans World Airlines flight menus, started a search for an illustrator who could create an image with the same look. He saw the illustration that I had commissioned from Sanders for the first part of the romantic serial which was set in New York City. He also saw a selection of Sanders' work covering nearly four decades of his career that I had produced for Leif Peng's *Today's Inspiration* illustration blog, and decided that Sanders was the man for the job, and asked him to work in his sixties style to create a series of illustrations.

Educated at St Olave's Grammar School, which then stood at the foot of London's Tower Bridge, Sanders spent much of his final year life drawing and painting at the Sir John Cass College of Art, less than a mile away on

43

ABOVE: The Artist As
A Young Man, thinking up
ideas for his personal
Christmas card. The only
piece that he kept
from his pre 1960
professional work.
ABOVE RIGHT: Through
experience Sanders has
learned that some people
who might object to
being photographed,
don't mind being drawn.

the other side of the river. He was offered a place at the Slade School of Art, but because of family circumstances he went to work in an advertising agency.

Sanders represented himself, and he got commissions from *Lilliput* Magazine, which he jokingly asserts he helped to close. Miles Huddlestone at Heinemann came to his rescue, giving him numerous book jacket commissions, which helped to keep the wolf from the door. He learned that most of the magazine's artwork was commissioned from two London artists' agents, and he joined one of them as a 'gofer'. It was in 1959 when Artist Partners took him onto their books, and put him on the road to success. They exposed him to sixty world-class artists and photographers and their work, and he says that he owes much to the help that many of them gave him.

His career was interrupted by National Service with the Royal Marines, mostly spent on active service with 45 Commando in areas of North Africa, and the Mediterranean. During his final year he was recruited into the Intelligence Section because of his drawing skills. After National Service he worked with photographer Adrian Flowers, to whom he is very grateful for the assistance he got in helping him to start his career. Sanders spent most evenings after work drawing, and a year later he selected his best twelve pieces for his portfolio, and went freelance. Flowers provided him

with a studio within his own studio in Chelsea, as a quid pro quo for background painting and visualizing.

Heavily influenced by the works of Ben Shahn and David Stone Martin, he found it difficult to advance stylistically away from what they did so brilliantly. Much to Artist Partners' consternation, he collected his samples, destroying all bar the one of him preparing ideas for his first printed Christmas card in 1959. He went drawing in a breaker's yard at the Elephant and Castle in south London, and at Billingsgate Fish Market, which was then between London and Tower Bridges— the stamping ground of his youth.

In the early 1960s, the American illustrator Bernie Fuchs was rapidly becoming the man to watch and emulate. In particular, the British art directors and illustrators were fascinated with what they called the "bubble and streak" style; but we had no idea how the Americans achieved it. Sanders used soap mixed with gouache in an attempt to get the paint to bubble, but to no effect. However, he achieved some success drawing in pencil or charcoal on canvas paper, scumbled with coloured inks mixed with soap, and worked over in gouache. There was then a *eureka* moment when we discovered Liquitex acrylic paints and mediums, which were manufactured in America. However, they weren't on sale in the United Kingdom, but it wasn't long before parcels of the paint and mediums were winging their

ABOVE: A portrait of Sanders' eldest son Mark, showing a keen interest in a worm. Always interested in science and biology and now in his early 50s, he works in the radiology department of a New Zealand hospital. Sanders early paintings emphasise texture and negative space, rather than attention to photographic detail.

way over the Atlantic, sent by friends and relatives.

I always admired Joy Hannington's work as the art editor of *Homes and Gardens* magazine; in particular the way she encouraged illustrators, giving them considerable freedom to work in the way which most suited them. She encouraged Sanders to develop his "bubble and streak" style, and he is grateful for the confidence she showed in him, and for the opportunities that followed. *Reader's Digest* also began to give him work, and he formed a working friendship with its art director Ken Ellis, which lasted until Ellis' death forty-five years later.

During the 1960s, Sanders' work was being used in all of the newspaper colour supplements, including the *Telegraph Magazine,* the *Observer Colour Supplement,* and *The Sunday Times Magazine.* The supplements gave illustrators excellent shop windows for their work. *The Sunday Times Magazine* art director was the brilliant and trail-blazing Michael Rand, who commissioned Sanders to illustrate the best shots made by ten great tennis players. He also asked Michael Leonard to paint several personalities, including Brigitte Bardot, which subsequently proved to be remarkably prescient, showing

what they might look like in later life. He then asked Sanders to produced a series of paintings illustrating what personalities looked like when they were young, and what they did for a living. They featured Eugene McCarthy, Ho Chi Minh, Kwame Nkrummah, Len Deighton, and Dame Edith Evans.

Sanders had made a series of experimental collages that helped persuade Stanley Kubrick to offer him the opportunity of recording the making of *2001: A Space Odyssey*. He drew on the set for two days each week, working on larger paintings in his studio. Although he worked on the project for more than a year, he only has a record of twenty-four of his works. He thinks that there may be more in the Kubrick Archive. Only two of these drawings were published before Kubick's death, and then not until 2001.

It was an exciting time, and many of the illustrators started to develop their highly individual styles, which reflected the fashions, music and arts at the time. However, In common with the illustrators working in the USA, the 1970s proved to be a challenging decade for every illustrator working in Britain, trying to

FACING PAGE: Homes and Garden's art editor, Joy Hannington had been expecting a horizontal half page but didn't complain when Sanders delivered this vertical illustration. ABOVE LEFT: His agent, Artist Partners, wanted an illustration which would appeal to the advertising industry. Sanders says, "MadMen? We lived the London equivalent, as Artist Partners' offices were in Mayfair, the centre of the advertising industry". ABOVE: 'The Red Geraniums'. The first illustration Joy Hannington of *Homes and Gardens* commissioned from Sanders, was a stark 'kitchen sink' story about two old people. This was the second.

ABOVE: One of Sanders'
concept paintings for
'2001 A Space Odyssey'.
The original was four feet square.
ABOVE RIGHT: This was painted
for the American market. The
artist thinks it was for art director
Bill Cadge at *Redbook*.
RIGHT: One of the only two pieces
of Sanders' '2001' concept art
published before the film
was released.
CENTRE RIGHT: An early
experiment in
"split screen" illustration.
FAR RIGHT: Illustration
for Sweden's *Damernas World*.

THE SINGING RAIN

BY HONORIA TIRBUTT

ILLUSTRATION BY BRIAN SANDERS

FOR the lonely ones in cities winter is a strange and desolate time. Among the tall buildings and the many-eyed blocks of flats the dusk slips blue and shadowy. Lights bloom sudden and mysterious, exotic golden blossoms suspended in the sky, rain blows light and chill along the pavements. Men and women move quickly now, blurred into dream faces in the early twilight.

Francesca paused in front of a lighted store. Her own image looked back at her, vague and wavering, the face a misty blur, the long fair hair twisted up in a knot. It was past closing time; the streets were almost deserted. Scraps of paper whipped along the gutters; buses ground past full of home-going faces. Somewhere over the high buildings a clock struck the hour. She tucked the violin case securely under her arm and moved away again; the skirts of her tweed coat blew against her, a shadowy, indeterminate figure in the pale evening, another student going home.

In the side streets the houses, tall and dim, retained an air of past grandeur, still with their pillars and porticoes. Francesca's fingers were cold as she took the key from her pocket. She had left her gloves somewhere again—she scattered a little trail of belongings as she moved daily between her lodgings and the college, a library

FRANCESCA WAS YOUNG AND IN LOVE BUT
SHE DREAMT OF MUSIC AND ROME

ABOVE TOP: 'The Singing Rain'. The final illustration was produced using ink and gouache.
ABOVE: An early acrylic double spread for *Woman* magazine. Sanders tried whenever possible to make the locations in the compositions as important as the figures.
FACING PAGE: Another job for *Homes and Gardens*. It was always Sanders aim to avoid the "clinch cliché".

pursue careers in magazine illustration. Television stole away advertising revenue and page counts went down. There was a decline in the interest in fiction in women's magazines, and for some reason art directors and art editors started asking the illustrators to produce more highly finished work. They also increasingly turned to photography in place of illustration. However, the market for paperback book cover illustration remained buoyant, although more and more photographic cover illustrations were being used.

It was also a time of personal change for Sanders. He felt that the scumbled acrylic (bubble and streak) style of illustration had run its course, and that the work of many illustrators was taking on a similar look. Knowing that figurative illustration was his forte, he began working with traditional methods, beginning with watercolour, as taught to him by his earliest mentor, J. C. Middleton, who had been art master at the school he had attended as a boy.

At the beginning of the 1970s, there was still a common belief in the graphics industry that watercolour was "wishy-washy" and did not reproduce well. His response was "You just need to charge your brush with more colour and allow for the fact that it dries a couple of tones paler than it looks when wet." There followed a series of magazine illustrations and paperback book covers, fully showing his mastery of the technique. However, he still

ABOVE: Double page spread for *Woman's Own*
FACING PAGE: Illustration for *Woman's Realm* circa 1970. Sanders got out his watercolours and embarked on further change. His agent said: "watercolour is too weak for reproduction." Ha!

did some illustrations using acrylics, including paintings of Cleopatra and Ophelia, which were commissioned as *Shakespeare for Schools* posters, published by *The Sunday Times*. In the early seventies, David Larkin, then art editor of Pan Books, asked Sanders if he would like to re-jacket their series of Steinbeck books. They both agreed that the medium of watercolour was too "English" for the subject matter, so it was agreed that he would work in acrylic using more solid colour. He thought that there were only six books, but was pleased to learn that there were in fact twenty-six.

At the end of the seventies, Sanders started producing artwork to be reproduced as postage stamps. The first Royal Mail set *Police* was begun in 1978 and published in 1979. The Royal Mail's commissioning art director Stuart Rose had seen Sanders' watercolour work in several magazines, and asked to see his portfolio. At the first meeting Sanders was surprised to learn that he was expected to work only four times larger than a printed stamp. Most of his work was large in scale, made to

reduce to page or double page spread magazine format. However, he took up the challenge, soon learning that good composition works at any size, but inevitably, at that small size, the artwork becomes tighter.

Having spent several weeks researching with the police on streets, motorways and river patrols, so he could produce a series of working drawings, he nearly lost the commission at the presentation stage by declining the Metropolitan Police's request to replace the mounted policewoman with a man. His small show of feminist solidarity might well have altered his career prospects, for in those days there was always a three-way competition for each set of British stamps. However, the art director's assistant, Barry Robinson, smoothed ruffled feathers; steered the work through the large stamp selection committee, and the set was chosen. Their working friendship lasted over the years until Robinson retired.

For his second set featuring *The Fishing Industry* in 1981, he toured the coast of Britain where he discovered an industry in decline, but met many entertaining characters, particularly in the north west of Scotland.

His third set illustrating *Youth Movements,* made in 1982, was the first time he designed four stamps that worked well as a set. His fourth set for the British Council which he produced in 1984, was designed by the Newell and Sorrel Design Group, with him executing the final artwork.

In 1985, he went from the miniature, to making a watercolour of HM Queen's presentation of new standards to the Royal Tank Regiment then stationed in West Germany, which measured six by four feet. In the same year he prepared in small scale *The Royal Air Force* stamps, which were published in 1986.

1987 saw the publication of a set for Guernsey Post Office featuring Guernsey born Sir Edmund Andros, who later became Governor of Virginia, Boston, and New Amsterdam—before it was renamed New York.

Having made first day cover cachets to all of his Royal Mail stamps for Unicover in the USA, the corporation

FACING PAGE: The cover art to 'Of Mice and Men', one of twenty six acrylic artworks that Sanders created for Pan Books series of John Steinbeck books. Art directed by David Larkin.

ABOVE: *Woman's Own*. Peter Lawrence was a very trusting young art editor who let Sanders go straight to finished artwork. Sanders thought he had pushed his luck by drawing back views of the girls, but it got it past the editor.

ABOVE TOP: Opening spread for a *Woman's Own* serial.
ABOVE: 'Taxis of the Marne'. General Galieni requisitioned the Renault taxis of Paris to take troops to the front in 1914. From 'Man and the Automobile' published in France as L'Homme et L'Automobile.

went on to commission him in 1988, to work on a fifty-year anniversary project *The History of World War 2 in Postage Stamps,* which was a massive undertaking, spread over five years, and which involved eight other artists. Of the one hundred issues, Sanders executed thirty-nine sets, which finally totaled eighty-two stamps. Each artwork was designed to include not only the stamp format, but the square shape of a 1st day cover cachet for each stamp. This complicated the design, as some stamps were printed in pairs or fours. Later the artwork was exhibited at The Imperial War Museum Cambridge.

During 1997 and 1998 he designed a further twenty-six stamps, and thirty-two coins for the Marshal Islands commissioned by Unicover on the subject of legendary fighting ships. Eight coins were minted as a separate set entitled *Legendary Fighting Ships of the US Navy.*

In 2000, he designed seven stamps and first day covers which honoured Sir Winston Churchill, and in 2004, a further eight stamps; a book of stamps, and a 1st day cover commemorating the end of World War 2 for the Isle of Man Post Office. In 2005, The Marshal Islands also re-issued *Historic Fighting Ships,* and two sets from the *The History of World War 2 in Postage Stamps* series.

Sanders has exhibited widely in mixed exhibitions, and

has had one man shows at The Imperial War Museum, York Castle Museum, The Association of Illustrators' Gallery, National Trust Gallery at Trelissic in Cornwall, and The Sir Rowland Hill Museum.

He has now been a professional artist for five decades, during which time he has worked in every area of the illustrative arts, ranging through book publishing, magazines, advertising, government agencies, film, television, and art education. He is one of the founders of the British Association of Illustrators.

In partnership with his wife, the illustrator Lizzie Sanders, who is also a paper engineer, he has produced many 3D paper works including *An Edwardian Doll's House,* and an accurately detailed paper model of Stonehenge, the prehistoric monument located in Wiltshire. He also executed the artwork for a large-scale pop-up model, and other illustrations of the ship, for a recent book about the Titanic.

During World War Two, together with thousands of other children living in London, who were evacuated to the countryside to protect them from Hitler's bombing campaign, he was sent to Saffron Walden, a charming market town in north Essex, where he and Lizzie now

ABOVE TOP: 'Rolls Royce Silver Ghost'. Sanders's work on this commission involved a considerable amount of research which certainly shows in these examples.
ABOVE: 'The Auburn'.
All of the illustrations for 'Man and the Automobile' were painted in acrylics.

Text continues on page 63

RIGHT: Sanders re-jacketed several C. S. Forester books for David Larkin at Pan. This was for 'Hornblower in the West Indies'.

FACING PAGE TOP: Article on duelling for *Men Only*. Sanders visited London's Hampstead Heath at dawn for the scene described by the author. As the mist cleared he saw a hawk stoop and take a pigeon.

BELOW: Packaging for Coty Products. 12 different packs were created from this artwork.

BELOW RIGHT: 'The Luck of Ginger Coffey'. Cover for a Brian Moore novel, published by Paladin.

BELOW FACING PAGE: One of more than thirty illustrations he made for James Herriot stories for various clients.

BELOW FACING PAGE RIGHT: 'The Emperor of Ice Cream', another of Sanders' book jackets for Paladin's Brian Moore novels.

A selection of Brian Sanders' stamps and coins for the 'Legendary Fighting Ships' series. First issued 1998 by the Marshal Islands and re-issued 2005 for the 200th anniversary of the Battle of Trafalgar. 35 full colour works were designed for use as stamps, first day covers and coins.
RIGHT: From the top: Bonhomme Richard. Brass coin. Ming Treasure Ship. Silver coin. USS Missouri. Silver coin.
FAR RIGHT: Clockwise: Trireme Romano. A highly maneuverable warship, with up to three banks of oars and a heavy bronze ram at the prow. Viking Longship. The first shield shows the cap badge of Sanders' old school St Olave's, named for King Olaf Haraldson of Norway who destroyed the Roman London Bridge by tying his ships to its supports and rowing downstream. USS Olympia, the Flagship of Admiral Dewy who in 1898 engaged and destroyed the Spanish Fleet off Manila Bay. USS Louisville final artwork. In 1991 the Louisville made the first ever submerged cruise missile strike in operation Desert Storm.

ABOVE: The sinking of the Bismark, art for one of two stamp pairs from 'The History of World War 2 in Postage Stamps.

RIGHT: More artwork from the World War 2 series of stamps which was commissioned in 1988 to coincide with the 50th anniversary of the war.

CLOCKWISE: 'The Fall of Singapore'. Artwork for stamp and 1st day cover

'First Combat of the Flying Tigers'.

'The Raid on St Nazaire U-Boat Pens'. HMS Cambletown rammed the lock gates with 3 tons of explosives in her prow, which exploded the following day disabling the harbour for the rest of the war.

Battle of El Alamein. Artwork for stamp and 1st day cover featuring General Montgomery 8th Army, and Field Marshal Rommel Afrika Corps.

FACING PAGE: The cover of the first of a biographical graphic trilogy covering the first twenty years of Sanders' life.

BRIAN SANDERS

Text continued from page 57

live in a village close by.

His most recently published book, *Evacuee: A Wartime Childhood,* the first in a biographical trilogy, which quotes him as saying; "I always wanted to be an artist and I'm still trying". It is a brilliantly written and illustrated book, evoking the atmosphere of wartime Britain. I was also a child at the time, but living in a different part of Essex, and his book brought back so many memories of a strange and threatening time, but also a time of joy and fascination. The adult view at the time was that the American GIs were "Overpaid, over-sexed and over here", and indeed many of them were a source of interest to many of the young British females at the time. They were definitely of interest to many of us young boys with their stories of life in America, and in the US forces; their chewing gum and chocolate were pretty good as well!

Sanders is now half way through producing the second part of the trilogy, and at seventy-five years-of-age he still works as hard as ever. ●

● *Sanders can be contacted through: **www.artistpartners.com** and by e-mail at: **briansanders.art@googlemail.com***

Janet and Anne Grahame Johnstone

Peter Richardson tells the story of the twin sisters whose combined talents created some of the most captivating artwork to ever grace the pages of children's literature.

IN 1979, WHEN THE WORK of Janet and Anne Grahame Johnstone presented a familiar and reassuringly ubiquitous face to the world of children's book publishing, an event occurred which threatened to destroy the career that the twin sisters had built up over the preceding quarter of a century. While the exact circumstances of the disaster remain unclear, what is known is that, as a result of a kitchen fire in their Suffolk home, Janet Johnstone succumbed to smoke inhalation, leaving Anne alone to carry on the work that they had jointly created since they were children. Anne's grief was compounded with the realisation that she would now have to master all the elements of the illustration that Janet had specialised in, and that she alone would have to be aide and confidante to their elderly mother Doris, who the twins shared their home with.

The story of the Johnstone twins is fascinating, as it is not only singular in regard to the closeness of their creative collaboration, which involved each of the sisters applying

ABOVE TOP AND FACING PAGE:
Illustrations for *Robin* comic which
the twins provided on a regular basis
from the title's debut in 1953.
ABOVE: 'Bill and Ben' the twins not
only drew the strip for *Robin*
comic but also devised the puppets
for the BBC TV show.

their particular skills to the elements of each of the artworks
they co-created, but it also reveals just how profound an
influence their mother's creativity had on the twins work.

Doris Zinkeisen was the eldest daughter of Victor Zinkeisen
a well to do shipper and yarn merchant and Clara Bolton Charles.
Victor's parents had arrived in Scotland in 1859 from Altenburg
in Thuringia, East Germany. The aura of an exotic hinterland
that the Zinkeisen surname bestowed seemed to perfectly
accord with the artwork that she and her younger sister Anna
produced to increasing acclaim throughout the 1920s and 1930s.
Doris' stage and costume design adding to her already enviable
reputation as a leading society portrait painter.

It was hardly surprising therefore that the stimuli that
had provided such a powerful creative spur to Doris' work
should also manifest itself in the work of Janet and Anne, who
were born to Doris and her husband Grahame Johnstone on
the 1st of June 1928; Janet, always the more assertive of the
sisters, preceding the arrival of Anne by twenty minutes.
The delightful irony of their birth-date occurring under
the astrological sign of the Heavenly Twins was not lost on
the sisters, who would often jokingly refer to their zodiacal
status as further evidence of their oneness.

A painting of the twins by their mother perfectly
encapsulates the description of them by their brother Murray
as "being one and a half people rather than two", as the dark
hair framing the girl's faces seems to merge them into one
being. Their early years growing up in London were offset by

A Fairy Landscape

In this pretty fairyland picture there are eight hidden objects. See if you can find them. There are two snails, two grasshoppers, two ladybirds and two lizards.

ABOVE TOP: Self-portrait by the twins mother painted in 1929.
ABOVE: Portrait of the twins aged five painted in 1934 by their mother Doris Zinkeisen, accentuates the "oneness" of the girls.

time spent at the family's "little house" in Northamptonshire, where the twins were able to indulge their love of the rural life and the accompanying flora and fauna that so characterised much of their art. Their natural creativity manifested itself from an early age, during which they created home-made comics, and one effort involving the combined talents of Janet, Anne and Murray, entitled 'The Life of Ponies', prefigured the direction that much of their later artistic activity would take them. It is not surprising that their instinctive talent for art was encouraged and nurtured by their parents and that following the death of their father Grahame in 1946, their mother fully endorsed and facilitated their creativity as the girls set up a studio together at Doris' London flat, which provided a perfect entrée into commercial art upon their graduation from St Martin's School of Art.

As Britain entered the 1950s, the work available for talented and industrious illustrators was relatively plentiful with a renaissance in periodical publishing, after years of war time paper rationing, offering a broad range of commissions, the concomitant boom in magazine consumption, the girls rapidly found outlets for their combined talents. One of their first commissioners was Shirley Brieger, a commissioning editor at Hulton Press, whose recent huge success with the launch of *Eagle* comic had emboldened them to follow this with a succession of colour comics, including one aimed squarely at very young readers under the banner of *Robin*. Brieger was impressed by both the talent of the twins and their ability to invest every commission, no matter how small, with total dedication. As a consequence they became regular contributors to *Robin* from the title's debut on the 28th March 1953.

ABOVE TOP: 'The Water Babies' from *Robin* comic 1962 and the cover to the 1950 Heirloom Edition of the story.
ABOVE: 'The Death of King Rufus' from Ida Foulis's 'This Land of Kings', published in 1954.

THE
WATER BABIES

CHARLES KINGSLEY

Their first strips for the comic involved a neat symbiosis, of which its youthful audience would have been entirely unaware for not only were the twins drawing the exploits of *Bill and Ben* and *Andy Pandy*, but they had also been responsible for devising and designing the TV iterations of these characters on which the strips were based. BBC TV had launched their *Watch With Mother* series that very same year, and the rigours of working for modest fees and tight deadlines had provided the girls with a good grounding in the discipline and commitment required for working as commercial artists. In addition, the demands of having to conceptualise and design in the round helped inform the work that they were to create throughout their career. A talent that they had evidently inherited from their mother Doris, whose set design had gained her much acclaim.

Their earliest published work revealed their flair for the wildlife that Janet specialised in as well as the well-researched costume work, which was Anne's forte. Costume was a subject that both the girls had studied whilst at St Martin's, and again reflected their mother Doris' influence. Books such as Enid Blyton's 'Tales of Ancient Greece' and Ida Foulis' 'This Land of Kings' allowed them to indulge both these passions, but it was Dodie Smith's '101 Dalmatians' published in 1956 that brought their work to the attention of a much wider audience.

Their work beyond reflected a wide variety of influences. Closest to home, both geographically and contemporaneously, the influence of *Radio Times* doyen, Eric Fraser and Pauline Baynes (destined for fame as the illustrator of both C. S. Lewis's Narnia books and J. R. Tolkein's 'The Hobbit', looms large. Further afield, European fairy tale illustrators such as

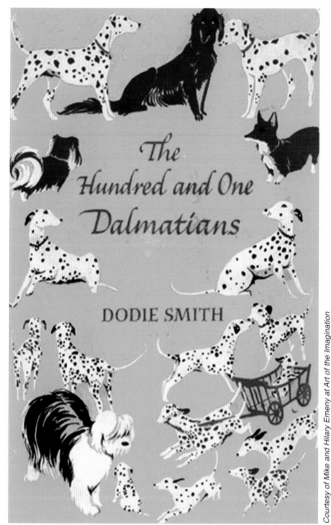

ABOVE: Artwork for 'The Black Whippet',
published in 1959 and Dodie Smith's
'101 Dalmatians', published in
1956 demonstrate the twins ability to invest
their animal illustration with as
much personality as their figure-work exudes.
RIGHT: Two original artworks for 'Dean's Book
of Nursery Rhymes', published 1965.

John Bauer and Kay Nielsen underscore much of their colour work, whilst the powerful graphics of ancient Greek pottery and medieval tapestry would also inform much of their output as their fame spread, and the commissions they commanded grew in scope and stature.

The success of '101 Dalmatians' proved something of an embarrassment for the author Dodie Smith, who finding it hard to reconcile the miserly flat fee of £100.00 which the twins received, paid Janet and Anne an additional £150.00 out of her own pocket and insisted on securing their talents for its sequels, the first of which, 'The Star Light Barking', was published some twelve years later, and for which they received £250.00.

Work for books by other popular children's writers such as Lorna Hill and Paul Gallico helped raise their profile even higher. Their atmospheric handling of black and white illustration, which had so enhanced '101 Dalmatians' was soon supplanted by their flawless colour work; the relative crudity of the colour plates from 'This Land of Kings' giving way to exquisitely painted pages where their strong design sense and eye for detail and costume took full advantage of increasingly accurate printing. With a move away from illustrations presented as individual colour plates set in a white frame with accompanying caption to full colour

O'ROSES

ONE FOR YOU AND ONE FOR

ULL OF POSIES

AND ONE FOR LITTLE MOSES

picture books with each artwork extending off the page, the Johnstone twins were ideally equipped to exploit these refinements to their full advantage.

Two commissioners in particular were at the forefront of maximising the potential reach that these advances in print technology now offered publishers. Dean & Son was one of the UK's oldest established publishers, their founder George Dean having exploited the use of commercial printing in 1800, two years after the Germans reduced the costs. The company's development and publishing of the first "pop-up" books in the 19th century had established them as one of the dominant UK publishers.

By the early 1960s Dean along with a lot of other publishers, including Hulton, had been swallowed up in a series of buyouts and takeovers. Hulton had already been absorbed by Odhams, which along with Dean & Son had become part of the IPC empire. So it was hardly surprising that with contacts from their Hulton days now operating out of IPC's Ludgate office (which still traded under the Dean & Son name) the sisters should find that their talents were once again being sought.

With work pouring in for what seemed like a never-ending series of Dean & Son's picture books devoted to classic fairy tales, nursery rhymes and children's prayers, the sisters

Courtesy of Mike and Hilary Emeny at Art of the Imagination

already had a very full schedule but this was by no means the sum total of the commissions that they were shouldering.

In 1962, the firm of Purnell had also come knocking on the door of the twins London studio. Like Dean, Purnell was a long established UK publisher having originated in the 19th century as the brain child of Charles Dando Purnell, a Methodist minister who was so concerned about rising unemployment in his village of Paulton in Somerset, that he set up a printing company. Purnell rapidly rose to become the pre-eminent publisher of Bibles, and the success of the company saw them grow to become one of the largest UK publishers, merging with Hazell Sun to form the British Printing Corporation (BPC) in 1964.

The call upon the talents of Janet and Anne was to provide artwork for serialisations of classic legends appearing in a new weekly children's magazine entitled *Finding Out*. Launched as a rival to IPC's hugely successful *Look and Learn*, *Finding Out* was to provide the catalyst for some of the twins most exciting and captivating artwork. Ever the pragmatists and utterly professional in the interpretation of their briefs, whilst the work that they provided for Dean's mass produced nursery books necessitated veering towards the sentimental, the work for Purnell, by contrast delved into darker themes. The twins responded to the texts written by Oxford academic and celebrated children's author, Roger Lancelyn Green with some of their most powerful work. The stories were collected

together in five volumes under the titles: 'Tales of the Greeks and Trojans', 'Myths from Many Lands', 'Folk Tales of the World', 'Sir Lancelot of the Lake' and 'Jason and the Golden Fleece'. The books are now highly sought after by collectors, as the illustrations contained are some of the most inspired artworks that the Grahame Johnstones produced throughout their long career. Drawing on relevant sources such as Greek pottery, and medieval tapestries and illuminations, the work that they created seemed to hark back to their mother's sense of theatre, lighting and staging.

The success that the twins enjoyed enabled them and their mother to move out of London and relocate to the rural Arcadia of Badingham, deep in the Suffolk countryside. Life at the White House enabled the women to indulge their love of pets in general, and equestrianism in particular, the sisters having inherited their mother's passion for carriage driving which had been a feature of much of Doris Zinkeisen's post-war painting. Cups and rosettes for their equestrian pursuits and the occasional foray from small ponies into their well appointed home added extra piquancy to afternoon tea with the Zinkeisen/Grahame Johnstones.

Despite this appearance of Bohemian eccentricity the demand for their work was so great that much of their day was devoted to keeping on top of their omnipresent deadlines. Close reading of texts, meetings with authors, research into costume and locale and careful consideration of reproducible

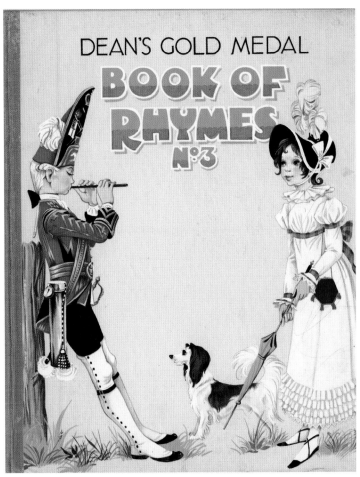

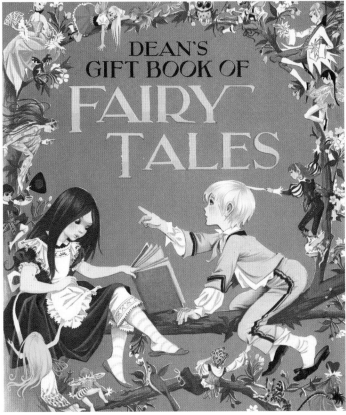

FACING PAGE: The endpapers to 'Dean's Gold Medal Book of Fairy Tales'. Published in 1964.
ABOVE TOP: Covers to two of the earliest Dean collections published in 1964 and 1967 respectively.
ABOVE: Endpapers to 'Dean's Book of Nursery Rhymes'. Published in 1967.
LEFT: Cover to 'Dean's Gift Book of Fairy Tales'. First published in 1967.

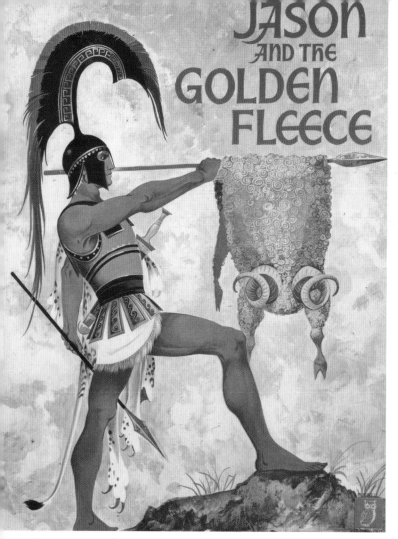

JASON AND THE GOLDEN FLEECE

Zeus

Poseidon

Hades

THE MODERN MAGAZINE FOR YOUNG PEOPLE EVERYWHERE   Every Monday 2/6   Vol. 15 No. 6

IAΣON

ABOVE AND FACING PAGE: *Finding Out* magazine was launched as a competitor to the children's educational magazine *Look and Learn*. Janet and Anne Grahame Johnstone were commissioned to illustrate a series of classic tales by Roger Lancelyn Greene. In the process they created some of their most powerful artworks to date.

colour schemes taking up much of their time before they got around to the demands of producing the commissioned artworks. From the time of their arrival at Badingham in 1966, they were on a veritable treadmill of commissions, the bulk of the work destined for Dean and Son's mass-produced books, whose outlets went well beyond the confines of bookshops and included newsagents and Woolworth's department store. With many of their books constantly reprinted and appearing in numerous translations, they were literally sharing their work with a worldwide audience of millions.

The universality of their appeal was such that the project management team of a proposed Danish Hans Christian Andersen themed tourist attraction approached the twins in 1976 with their proposal that Janet and Anne should undertake all the design work required for the venture. The amount of work entailed was truly prodigious, but undeterred, the twins committed themselves to six-year contracts and set about producing a vast array of ideas and designs for the park. Sadly the project foundered at the last minute, when the main financial backer got cold feet and withdrew his support for the venture.

The disappointment that the sisters experienced was, however, tempered with the knowledge that such was the demand for their work that their career would not be too greatly compromised by the abrupt termination of their contract. The greatest threat to their career lay three years down the line, and it was the unexpected death of Janet that

Janet Johnstone.

Anne Grahame Johnstone.

really did hold the potential to spell finis to the distinctive Grahame Johnstone style of illustration.

Janet's death presented Anne with the immediate need to assume full responsibility for producing the artwork that she and her twin had shared throughout their career, co-creating every illustration that they produced. Not only did this mean an effective doubling of the production time for each artwork with a concomitant diminution in the family income but added to these concerns was the necessity of having to master all the skills that Janet had specialised in, especially in the rendering of animals and horses. On a more practical front there was also the requirement for Anne to take driving lessons, as Janet had been the sole driver in the household, and on top of all those other worries was the knowledge that she alone was now responsible for ministering to the needs of their now elderly mother.

It was a real testament to the grit and determination of Anne that she was able to overcome challenges, which at first glance might have seemed insurmountable. With the initial assistance of Doris, she was able to master the depiction of horses, and her commissions included some breath-taking work for Jane Carruth's re-telling of Charles Kingsley's 'The Water Babies' and J. M. Barrie's 'Peter Pan'. Sadly, as Doris

grew older and less inclined to either visit or receive visitors, so Anne's life became progressively more circumscribed, to the point that most of her maintenance of old friendships was conducted via letter, her daily companions being Doris and the numerous pets that inhabited the house and grounds of their home.

Doris Zinkeisen died in 1991. Anne was diagnosed with cancer of the liver a few years later, but continued to paint until two days before her death on the 25th May 1998, so ending one of the most remarkable and unusual careers in British illustration.●

We would like to extend our thanks to Philip Kelleway for allowing us to draw on much of the information on the Zinkeisen family, which appears in his excellent book; 'Highly Desirable: The Zinkeisen Sisters & Their Legacy', a review of which appears on page 94 of this issue. Thanks also to Hannah Izod of *The Seven Stories Collection* for all her assistance as well as Phil Rushton and David Slinn for supplying scans of the twins early work. In addition we would like to thank Mike and Hilary Emeny of *Art of the Imagination* for supplying scans of all the original artworks that appear throughout this feature.

FACING PAGE: With echoes of European fantasy painters such as Hieronymous Bosch and Pieter Bruegel the Elder, an unidentified original painting showing both the sisters signatures, explores darker themes than was the norm for much of their commercial work.

ABOVE: After the death of her sister Janet, Anne Grahame Johnstone continued working developing a "hyper-realist" approach to her painting, where strands of hair and blades of grass would be rendered with exquisite care, as this card illustration from 1986 reveals.

Derek Eyles

David Ashford recalls the life and times of one of the greatest portrayers of horses and horsemen in action.

© IPC Media

© IPC Media

ABOVE: 'Thunder on the Prairie'. Eyles captures the excitement and spectacle of the Wild West in this illustration for the endpapers of the *Kit Carson Cowboy Annual 1959*.

THE GREAT HOLLYWOOD WESTERN STAR, Gary Cooper, once remarked, "One of the most beautiful sights in the world is a running horse, with a man who sits on it real pretty". I'm sure that Derek Eyles would have been in complete agreement with him. No British illustrator drew horses and horsemen more often than Eyles—or drew them more convincingly. All his finest images contain horses, whether it is a highwayman galloping down a moonlit road, Red Indian braves riding on the warpath, or a cowboy turning in the saddle to fire at his pursuers. Such was his expertise that, when he was working for Britain's foremost comic publisher, the Amalgamated Press, a directive was issued that all artists who needed to improve their drawing of horses should be sent examples of his work.

Derek Charles Eyles was born in North Finchley, London, in 1902, the son of Charles Eyles, an artist who had worked with the Impressionists in Paris, and who himself later painted a few covers for children's annuals. Derek

Eyles married in his twenties, and in 1929, his son John was born. John also exhibited artistic leanings but pursued a career in teaching, eventually marrying an Italian and moving to Italy, where he died at the early age of forty-eight as a result of an unsuccessful kidney operation.

All through the 1920s, '30s and '40s, Eyles contributed illustrations and book covers for novels, annuals and story papers. He worked for a myriad of different publishers, and it would be a most daunting task not only to list all the books he illustrated, but all the publishers for whom he worked. Throughout the 1930s and '40s, Eyles painted innumerable covers for novels featuring tales of his beloved American West and, even as late as 1951, he was painting covers for Pearson's Western Novels. In contrast to the pulp covers which he saved as reference, there is a certain gentility to be found in his work that lends a more romantic glow to it than that found in the US pulps. His superbly drawn horses tend to look more like

ABOVE LEFT: A painting by Eyles published in the *Knockout Fun Book 1951*, depicts Kit Carson pursued by some particularly irascible "injuns".
ABOVE: A very early Eyles illustration, from *Chums* in the 1920s, reveals a much more impressionistic approach to his painting.

ABOVE TOP: Eyles had a particular affinity for the era of stage coaches and highwaymen. His researches into the subject infused his artwork with added authority as well as the innate sense of dynamics he brought to his art.
ABOVE: Young gentlemen playing football, typical of the fare that Eyles was supplying to publishers throughout the 1930s.
FACING PAGE: Scanned from the original art, Kit Carson in yet another contretemps with Native Americans.

thoroughbreds than the stocky cow pony of reality.

In the early 1930s, Eyles illustrated a number of large format children's books, including Lamb's 'Tales from Shakespeare' for Hutchinson, and two books about King Arthur: 'Knights of the Round Table' for Collins and 'King Arthur and his Knights' for The Children's Press. These delightful books were profusely illustrated, including full colour plates as well as black and white drawings, and a wrap-around dust jacket. During that time he was kept very busy supplying covers for such publishers as Collins 'Adventure Annual', Warne 'Adventure Book for Boys', Oxford 'Big Book for Boys', and Dean 'Monster Book for Boys'. On occasions, he supplied black and white line drawings as well, which helped to liven up what were fairly dull volumes.

During this time, he was also illustrating for the magazines of the day, notably the *Wide World Magazine,* to which he was contributing as early as 1924. These illustrations were printed in half-tone, and it is interesting to see that this very early work, obviously influenced by his father, is almost Impressionistic with its loose brush strokes, very different to the work he was to produce later.

Looking at one of Eyles' early 1920s' painting of cowboys having a fight in a corral, it can be seen that it was executed in oils, and is extremely free and very far removed from the work he was to do later. It is almost certain that this picture appeared as a colour plate in a *Chums Annual.* Looking carefully at other *Chums* plates by Eyles, it can be seen that they were all painted in oils and show that, like the Impressionists, he was thinking at this time in terms of tone rather than line. However, the reproductions in these *Chums Annuals* are not of great quality and it is easy to see why he may have decided to abandon this free, painterly style in favour of a much more linear technique that would reproduce more effectively. Only a decade later, this

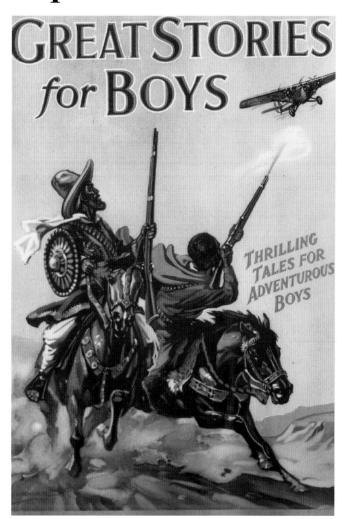

ABOVE: Cover and interior to one of the many collections of boy's adventure books that Eyles illustrated throughout the 1930s, it was during these years that Eyles developed his painting technique, which was far more attuned to working within the limitations of commercial printing.
FACING PAGE: 'Riding a Hobby Horse', another example of Eyles historical illustration, much of which was centred around highway adventures' with coach and horses well to the fore.
FACING PAGE FAR RIGHT: Buffalo Bill from *Kit Carson's Cowboy Annual 1954*.

new way of working is revealed in the many covers he contributed to the *Scout,* and was to become the painting style he would use in all his colour illustrations for the remainder of his career.

Derek Eyles worked in comics through the influence of a young man named Edward Holmes, who had been editing *Wild West Weekly,* which ran for just fifty issues from 1938 to 1939. The covers, particularly those by Eric Parker and Eyles, were vivid and colourful. During *Wild West Weekly's* short life, Holmes was busy editing another paper, a comic called *Knock-Out* [sic]. Pleased with the work they had been doing on his Western paper, Holmes made Eyles and Parker the comic's regular 'spot' illustrators.

Holmes had persuaded Parker to start drawing strips for *Knock-Out* as early as 1940, but it was not until 1947 that Eyles agreed to try his hand at the medium. He found that he took to it with consummate ease. Not surprisingly, his first picture strip was a Western, 'The Phantom Sheriff'. This character was no stranger to Eyles, as he had painted a number of covers featuring this masked lawman for *Wild West Weekly,* and he did a very good job.

Just a year later, he produced what many consider to be his finest work for comics, 'Dick Turpin's Ride to York', a romantic highwayman adventure told in a well-crafted picture strip that was not only full of non-stop thrills, but also historically accurate in detail and atmosphere. Eyles drew only one more strip for the comic, now spelled *Knockout;* a complete two-

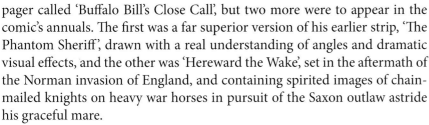

pager called 'Buffalo Bill's Close Call', but two more were to appear in the comic's annuals. The first was a far superior version of his earlier strip, 'The Phantom Sheriff', drawn with a real understanding of angles and dramatic visual effects, and the other was 'Hereward the Wake', set in the aftermath of the Norman invasion of England, and containing spirited images of chain-mailed knights on heavy war horses in pursuit of the Saxon outlaw astride his graceful mare.

A new type of British comic appeared in April 1950: the pocket-book size library format devoted entirely to adventure picture strips. The first of these was the *Cowboy Comics Library*, and Eyles' work appeared in the first *Kit Carson* issue. His stunning pen work convincingly conveyed the movement of covered wagons as they trundled across the great prairies; the savage majesty of painted Red Indian warriors on the warpath, and the heroism of the US Cavalry as they charged to the rescue, or gallantly defended their isolated desert fort. In the same year, another pocket size publication appeared, this time all text, called *The Western Library*, for which he painted some splendid covers.

When the Amalgamated Press decided to publish their first Western annual, it was not surprising that Eyles' work featured strongly—in fact, it could be said to be an all-Eyles' book. That first *Kit Carson's Cowboy Annual* contained four colour plates, all painted by Eyles. He also illustrated the cover, the title page, the editor's foreword and all the text stories. He

ABOVE TOP: 'Dick Turpin's Ride To York', was published in the weekly comic *Knockout*, and firmly established Eyles as one of the UK's leading comic artists. ABOVE: Eyles, although extremely disciplined in his commitment to meeting deadlines, was never a slave to his work and would often eschew comic strip assignments in favour of preserving free time for his other passions, such as building and sailing model boats. The photo above reveals a very dapper Eyles with one of his model boats at the Round Lake in Kensington Gardens from July 1949.

had drawn the leading strip specifically for the annual, but his other two strips were larger scale reprints of work that had appeared in early issues of Cowboy Comics. There were six more issues of the *Kit Carson's Cowboy Annual*, and all had covers painted by Eyles, apart from the 1958 issue which, however, did contain three Eyles colour plates.

Colleagues who knew him in the decades after the War were united in thinking that he was not exactly a workaholic. Editors found it difficult to make him work any harder than he felt was necessary. And strip work—with all those pictures—looked very much like hard work to him! His major strips, 'Dick Turpin's Ride to York', 'The Phantom Sheriff', 'Hereward the Wake', and his adventures of *Kit Carson* for the *Cowboy Comics Library*, are all executed with a pen. Leonard Matthews, the great Amalgamated Press editor, who had scripted most of Eyles' best strips, told me that 'Dick Turpin's Ride to York', which had run for just nine weeks when it was first published, had originally been scheduled to run to twenty-one weeks. Eyles, however, had found the work too demanding. As Matthews said, "Derek's argument was that, because he'd got to turn it out every week, he couldn't sail his boat in the park pond!" Nevertheless, as Matthews also said, "Derek really put his heart and soul into it".

Six years later, Matthews arranged for these nine installments to be expanded and altered to make up twenty episodes for the Sun comic. Although it was certainly well drawn, it cannot be compared to the work Eyles did on the original nine installments for *Knockout*. For the original *Knockout* strip, Matthews had insisted that he used a pen, but for the later version Eyles used a brush. According to Matthews, "Derek didn't like drawing with a pen because it slowed him down. He was much happier slapping it on with a brush". Matthews said, "Derek was a master with a pen and, although his brushwork was very good indeed, it never

AH! IF ONLY TOM KING WERE WITH ME NOW!

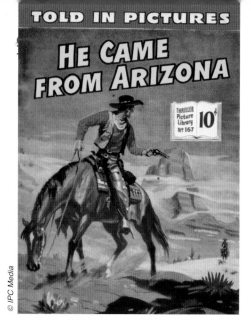

ABOVE: Original artwork and two covers for two 'Wild West' themed issues of *Thriller Comics Library*. Published from November 1951 to May 1963, the comic was one of the UK's most popular pocket libraries and featured regular attractions such as *Robin Hood* and *Buffalo Bill* as well as adaptations of classic novels such as 'Jane Eyre' and 'The Red Badge of Courage', much in the manner of U.S. publisher Gilberton's, *Classic Comics*.

approached the sheer excellence of his pen technique." Eyles was certainly not a prolific strip artist, and the appearance of an Eyles' strip was always something of an occasion. Throughout the 1950s, he illustrated a series of text stories by Joan Whitford writing under the pseudonym of Barry Ford featuring *Wild Bill Hickok* for the *Sun* comic, and the occasional cover pictures for the same comic featuring *Billy the Kid*, and its companion paper *Comet* featuring *Strongbow the Mohawk* and *Buffalo Bill*. He also contributed around forty-five covers for the *Thriller Comics Library*, as well as title pages featuring *Robin Hood* and *Wild Bill Hickok*, but only the one full-length strip: 'Crazy Horse, Warlord of the Sioux'. For the late issues of the *Cowboy Picture Library*, he drew three short strips and one full-length adventure for the *Davy Crockett* issues, and a total of six covers.

He began contributing a number of paintings to *Look and Learn* in the early sixties, as well as strips to *TV Comic* and the *TV Comic Annual*. Although obviously intended for a younger audience, his strips for the *TV Comic Annual,* which included stories of Vikings, Roundheads and Cavaliers, the Three Musketeers and, of course, cowboys and Indians, are full of verve

and dash. There was an obvious sense of enjoyment in this work, which can also be discerned in his series of paintings for large-scale jigsaw puzzles of cowboy subjects that he produced for Character Enterprises Ltd. in 1960.

During the latter part of the 1960s, Eyles was mostly working for the nursery end of the juvenile market and his inimitable style could be found in the beautifully printed, large format publication for young people called *Treasure*. For this paper he contributed full colour work of historical subjects and large, full-page landscape pictures, printed in two colours, illustrating and decorating poems. Widely known and respected as one of the finest horse artists around, it was only natural that his work was in demand for the girls' comic, *Princess*, and its annual, the *Princess Pony Book*. He was also responsible for the two-page strip in *TV Toyland* featuring *Champion the Wonder Horse*, as well as the colour back page strip version of *The Magic Boomerang*.

In the seventies, he began to experience problems getting work. It seemed that Westerns and other horseback adventures were no longer popular with the young, and there was more emphasis on war and horror in boys' comics. He said, "There's too much violence required now for my liking". Until the end of

ABOVE: Editor Leonard Matthews was to have a profound influence on the career of Derek Eyles With every new publication that the ever energetic Matthews launched, Eyles was amongst the first of his illustrators to be invited to contribute artwork. Original painting by Eyles' illustration depicting a tense moment from James Fenimore Cooper's 'Last of the Mohicans', first published in *Look and Learn* No. 15, 28th April 1962.

ABOVE TOP: 'Covers to the first two Kit Carson Cowboy Annuals, the bulk of which were illustrated by Eyles. **ABOVE:** Daydreaming, an illustration which encapsulates Eyles ability to capture a boy's imagination.

the 1930s, Eyles had devoted himself to book illustration. He had designed covers and contributed other illustrations, sometimes in paint, and at other times in pen and ink, for every type of book available at the time. Then fate stepped in and turned him into an artist for the comics. Adventure strips featuring horsemen were all the rage in British comics at the time, particularly those with a Western theme, and here was the very man for that work. The two great editors at the Amalgamated Press, Edward Holmes and Leonard Matthews, both recognized his talent for just such romantic adventure strips. Matthews would insist on his artists looking closely at Eyles' work to discover how to draw horses. And Eyles' influence was not simply confined to the artists of the Amalgamated Press. When I wrote to the well-known illustrator, Harry Bishop, I mentioned the fact that a number of frames in his early *Gun Law* strips for *The Daily Express* were more or less copied from drawings and paintings by Eyles. He wrote back saying, "Yes, he did influence me. I loved his work, and as a boy I collected it and copied it whenever I could."

I met Derek Eyles in the autumn of 1974, just months before his death. I mentioned that I wanted to get in touch with another illustrator I rated highly, Eric Parker. Derek agreed that Parker was a very good adventure artist but added with a mischievous smile, "His horses weren't as good as mine though, were they?" ●

ILLUSTRATION

SUMMER 2013 ISSUE 36

Whether you collect incunabula, books by Eric Ravilious or Edward Ardizzone, vintage posters, comics, or Edward Gorey's postcards, it's all in *Illustration*.
E-mail info@illustration-mag.com,
phone 07900 698 124,
or visit www.illustration-mag.com.

RALPH STEADMAN: BEYOND GONZO

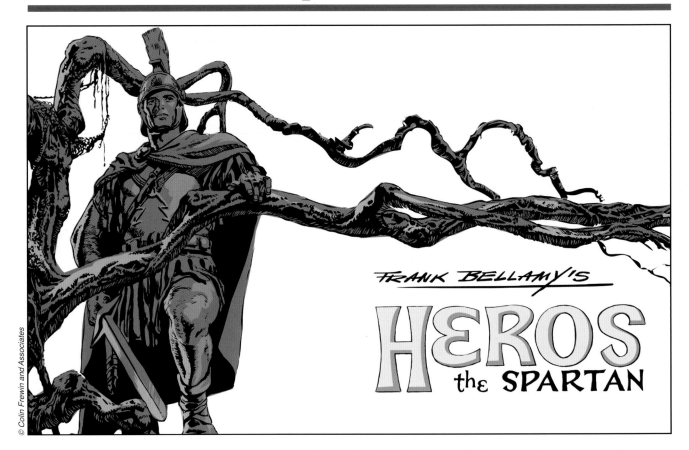

WHAT A FANTASTIC OPPORTUNITY FOR A teenage boy: Art editor Arthur Roberts gave me my first job in Fleet Street, as a lettering artist on the thinking childs' comics *Eagle, Girl, Swift* and *Robin*. The wages didn't matter much, I would get free copies of all Sir Edward Hulton's publications; the comics for me every week, *Picture Post* for my father, the monthly *Housewife* magazine for my mother, *Farmer's Weekly* for the gardener, and I'd get to meet all my heroes who did the illustrations. The staff were a pretty interesting bunch as well. My abiding memory of founding editor, the hard-drinking and chain-smoking Reverend Marcus Morris, was of white socks and suede shoes, and a daily trip by a messenger boy in a taxi to Hampstead, to collect important papers he'd forgotten to bring to the office. The most exotic woman I had ever seen was Jean Crouch, the editor of *Girl*, accompanied every day by two equally exotic dogs. Her deputy editor, John Trent, a colourful former Brighton College boy who, after achieving his ambition to live in California, met an early death in a car crash in Pasadena. In the general studio, Gerald Royston Lipman (Lip) the cartoonist, who went on to become cartoon editor of Express Newspapers, sat behind a pillar producing spot drawings every day for publication in each of the four comics, and there was Miss Tavener. I don't think any of us ever got to know her first name: she resembled Miss Marple as portrayed by Joan Hickson, and kept us youngsters in order with icy resolve and withering looks.

Marcus Morris, who became honorary chaplain of St Bride's, the journalists' church in Fleet Street, was concerned at the detrimental effects that imported American comics might have on British children. He and illustrator Frank Hampson assembled a team of artists and writers, and produced a dummy

FACING PAGE: The opening spread for Book Palace Books *Heros the Spartan*. This gigantic book measuring 36cms X 27cms presents each episode of Frank Bellamy's legendary strip at the same size it was originally published in the *Eagle*.
ABOVE: The first appearance of Heros; *Eagle* 27th October 1962.
LEFT: The artist photographed in 1972 with the artwork for a Doctor Who *Radio Times* cover on his lap.

ABOVE, RIGHT, AND FACING PAGE:
Developmental sketch and two pages
(the one on the facing page scanned from
the original artwork) of Frank Bellamy and
Clifford Makin's treatment of the story
of David. Bellamy's interpretation of *Eagle*
editor Marcus Morris's vision to bring
the Bible alive through the medium
of comics. Certainly, no other artist
could have fulfilled this brief with more
assurance than Bellamy brought
to each and every page of the story.

Hulton Press had a massive readers' letters department, which was for opening and answering all mail.
Q: Following 'David, the Shepherd King', you went on to 'Marco Polo', but only a few months later, you switched strips again to 'Dan Dare'. Why was this?
FB: Well, I think Frank Hampson was getting a bit tired of 'Dan Dare' by this time. So Marcus Morris, editor of *Eagle* at that time, asked me if I'd like to take over. I had a chat with Frank Hampson, who also wanted me to take over and, under the agreement that it would be for one year only, I started drawing 'Dan Dare'.
Q: Of course, Frank Hampson hadn't been the only artist to work on 'Dan Dare' before you took over. Did you move in with the "Hampson Team"?
FB: Yes. But quite a few changes had been made since the early days. Many of the scale models had gone. Some of the old artists had vanished too, and we were minus the photographic department. In fact, we were getting back to the straight forward strip drawing, with one artist doing one set of drawings, instead of as a team.
Q: Did it come as a relief to draw a strip like 'Dan Dare' that was complete fantasy after such projects as 'Churchill'?
FB: Well, yes and no. It never really frightened me, having to work from references, I found it enjoyable at times. But on the other hand, I did like the freedom of utter fantasy.
Q: But didn't you have to refer back to Frank Hampson's version quite a bit?
FB: Oh, yes. But drawing is like hand writing. It belongs to an individual so another person's is bound to be different. You can see a vast difference between Frank Hampson, Don Harley and Keith Watson's versions of 'Dan Dare'. To me the difference stands out like a sore thumb, even though the uniforms are the same. One interesting thing there, because they worked from photos a great deal, all the uniforms were actually made, and photos taken of people modelling them. It was all far removed from my normal

36

issue for a new weekly, the *Eagle.* He presented it to various publishers, and eventually Hulton Press agreed to publish it. The first issue went on sale in April 1950. Morris and his family lived in Surrey, and Hampson set up a studio in their house. In November 1951, Morris launched *Girl,* a girls' counterpart to the *Eagle,* which was followed by *Robin* in 1953, for younger children, and by *Swift* in 1954. Another cleric who was closely involved in the production of the comics was Anglican priest Edward Chad Varah, who supplemented his income by working as a script writer for *Eagle* and its sister publications; he also founded The Samaritans in 1953.

When one thinks of *Eagle,* Frank Hampson's strip of Dan Dare and the Mekon immediately spring to mind. However, Frank Bellamy who had worked for the comic producing 'The Happy Warrior', featuring the life of Winston Churchill, 'The Shepherd King', the life of the biblical King David, and 'The Travels of Marco Polo', amongst others, replaced Hampson and spent a year drawing Dan Dare, but his triumph for the comic was producing Heros the Spartan in 1962 and 1963.

Illustrators editor Peter Richardson has edited and designed a beautiful book entitled *Frank Bellamy's Heros the Spartan.* It was a privilege to be invited to do some minor production work on the book, and I thoroughly enjoyed seeing Bellamy's incredible artwork at close quarters once again. Richardson has excelled himself with the editing and in his powerful designs of introductory pages featuring Bellamy's drawings in monochrome, in contrast to page after page of colourful spreads, many of which have been scanned from the originals. There are forewords by John Byrne, Dave Gibbons, Walter Simonson, Ken Steacy, and John Watkiss, with an introduction by Norman Boyd, each giving their own views and insights into the working methods and life of this incredible artist. It is one of the best books of its kind that I have ever seen: pages and pages of pure joy. There must be plenty of us old codgers left who want to take this trip down memory lane, and I only hope that Geoff West, the publisher at Book Palace Books, has ordered enough copies to go round. *Bryn Havord* ●

HEROS BOOK 2

EAGLE MARCH 9TH 1963 – OCTOBER 26TH 1963

THE EAGLE OF THE FIFTH

In 'The Eagle of the Fifth', Tully and Bellamy take the dark themes already established in the preceding story, and weave a truly epic adventure, where barbarian hordes, jackal-men and sea monsters seem to threaten the very fabric of an Empire in decline. As if these concerns were not enough, Heros has to contend with conspiracies and betrayal which drive him and the doomed fifth legion into the maw of an implacable and ferocious enemy. The resultant spread which depicts the destruction of the Fifth Legion was exhibited at New York's Academy of Comic Book Arts in 1971, when Bellamy was awarded the prize for best foreign artist.

FACING PAGE: The introductory section of *Frank Bellamy's Heros the Spartan*, includes an interview with Bellamy that was conducted by Dez Skinn and Dave Gibbons in 1973 and remains the most comprehensive interview conducted with the artist.

ABOVE: Every spread of the original serialisation of Bellamy's Heros has been painstakingly scanned and restored, so that the pages of the comic look as fresh as the day they were originally published.

LEFT: Each of Bellamy's Heros stories include a brief introduction, which helps the reader contextualise the overall work.

● *Frank Bellamy's Heros the Spartan*
Limited edition of 600 copies. Hard Cover. 272 pp £95.00.
Leather Cover edition of 120 copies.
Hard Cover. 296 pp £265.00.

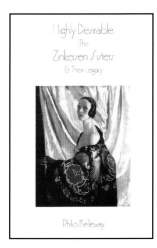

Lifestyle Illustration of the 50s
by Rian Hughes & David Roach
Softbound 512 pages.
Goodman Fiell £19.20/$33.50

The Fairest One Of All
by J. B. Kaufman.
Hard-bound 320 pages.
Aurum Press £22.40/$46.00

Highly Desirable—The Zinkeisen Sisters
by Philip Kelleway
Hard-bound 290 pages.
Leiston Press £47.75

IT IS A COLOURFUL BOOK. I was there back in the fifties commissioning the artists and designing fiction pages, so I wanted to like the book. I don't. The images were scanned from British magazines, so it is unfortunate that the editor has subjectively chosen so many works by Americans, and neglected some of the best English illustrators.

The page designs are monotonous, as if they are trying to bore the readers into submission, and the most ridiculous thing that I have ever seen in publishing is on page ten, where the whole page is devoted to a photograph of the blank back of a sheet of illustration board!

Hughes' decision to invite Anita Virgil, an American illustrator's widow, to describe how an artist works was bizarre, especially as I had arranged to take David Roach to lunch with Walter Wyles, a leading British illustrator in the fifties, so that he could interview him about his life and working practices. Roach didn't take up the offer.

Hughes recently said on Facebook "Love to do more books. Lots of ideas. I may have to reexamine [sic] the publisher options, though… open to offers"

I can hear the champagne corks popping at publishers Goodman Fiell.
— **Bryn Havord**

ITS HARD TO IMAGINE JUST how mind blowing the advent of the first full length animated feature was for the people that created it, and the crowds that queued for hours outside cinemas to witness the arrival of a film that would have seemed impossible a few years earlier.

J. B. Kaufman's text manages to plunge the reader back into those heady days. With recourse to the minutes of Disney storyboard meetings and interviews with the key personnel, the story of how Walt Disney and his team of young artists, actors, writers and musicians managed to create an animated film that has had the power to captivate generations of audiences makes for a truly compelling read.

Added to the reading experience is all the extra source material that Kaufman has included, which all add to the sense that while this book carries its learning lightly, putting across its story in an engaging and accessible manner, it is nevertheless the product of many years of unstinting research.

The book itself, is well designed and the artwork covering all aspects of the production of 'Snow White and the Seven Dwarfs' adds extra allure to a tale well told.
— **Peter Richardson**

FOR DEVOTEES OF Janet and Anne Grahame Johnstone's art, it may come as a surprise that their mother was also one of two highly talented sisters, who took the art world by storm in the 1920s and created a cult of celebrity around themselves long before Facebook and the Twittersphere became the default setting for self promotional networking.

Kelleway's text follows the lives and careers of Doris and Anna Zinkeisen as they set about applying their talents to portraiture, costume design, theatre design, and work in the film industry. Their talent and boundless energy was inherited by their children and Kelleway's researches follow the lives of the Zinkleisen sisters as well as their children and while Janet and Anne Grahame Johnstone carved out enviable careers for themselves as illustrators, their cousin Julia Heseltine (Anna Zinkeisen's daughter) became a noted portrait painter, as well as an accomplished landscape artist.

The author has done an admirable job in gaining access to friends and family of these remarkable artists. The book contains a generous selection of art and photographs which adds further lustre to this fascinating tale.
— **Peter Richardson**

It was with a degree of humility mixed with delight that we received the following two emails from Tarzan collector and afficionado Robert R. Barrett in response to the feature on Fortunino Matania:

Dear Sirs,

I just received a copy of *illustrators* three and read with interest Peter Richardson's essay on Fortunino Matania. I never seem to get enough information about Matania and his art. The reason for this email is to comment on something that Mr. Richardson wrote at the end of his essay:

"(Matania) was contacted by American art director Vern Coriell to provide artwork for a new edition of Edgar Rice Burroughs' Pirates of Venus and Lost On Venus. Coriell had not only seen the illustrations he had created for a previous serialization of these stories some twenty years earlier, but had also tracked down the originals and had them hanging framed on the walls of his home."

In truth Vern Coriell was not an art director. Instead he was a circus acrobat who created the fanzine *The Burroughs Bulletin* as well as the Burroughs Bibliophiles, a group of fans and collectors of the life and works of Edgar Rice Burroughs. In the 1950s, he and another Burroughs collector contacted Fortunino Matania and purchased all of his illustrations from the Burroughs Venus serials published in *The Passing Show*. Coriell did not commission Matania to create new illustrations for a new edition of the Venus stories. Vern Coriell did commission Matania to execute an oil painting for him in 1961, depicting a scene from Burroughs' A Princess of Mars.

Both Vern Coriell and the other collector passed away several years ago, and the Matania illustrations for the Venus serials passed on the collector's son and myself (sadly I kept only a few of the Venus illustrations, trading or selling some to finance new art acquisitions). I also acquired the Princess of Mars painting—one of the gems of my collection!

Thank you for a very fine magazine.
—**Robert R. Barrett**

Dear Peter,

Thank you for replying to my email, and I'm pleased that you will be able to correct that portion of your article dealing with Vern Coriell. I was amazed to learn that Matania only asked for eighty pounds sterling of Coriell for the Princess of Mars painting which, I believe was equivalent to approximately $US224 at that time.

Vern passed away in 1985, and his estranged wife sold Matania's Princess of Mars to another collector. I asked a good friend of mine who was acquainted with the collector if he would be interested in trading the Matania for a small Frazetta painting. The collector was so anxious to have the Frazetta painting that he immediately sent the Matania painting off and even included one of Matania's original Venus illustrations as part of the trade! While I hated to trade the Frazetta art, I wanted the Matania even more! Thank you for your kind comment regarding my Burroughs artist articles and the photo from Squa Tront. Frank set his camera up on a tripod, set the timing to give him enough time to sit down with us, and the camera went off. Frank then took the film out and took it to the basement where his darkroom was, and developed it so that I could have a print right away. Although the article was only the second that I had written for a fanzine it remains one of my favourites.

I don't know if you know the website *www.pulpartists.com*, but I was able to give some assistance to the owner of the site, David Saunders (whose father was the pulp cover artist Norman Saunders), on his entries on the lives of the Burroughs pulp artists.
—**Robert**

The photograph of Frank Frazetta (left), and Robert R. Barrett as it appeared in Squa Tront No.5 published in 1969.

Dear Peter,

Received *illustrators* three. Beautiful mag. You did me proud… thank you so much… I will show it off to the people at *The EuroWeekly News* to educate them how it was done by real Fleet Street people way before the computer. Writing, layout and presentation is superb.

Many thanks again.
—**Peter Maddocks**

Dear Mr Richardson,

Thank you so very much for the exquisite magazine with my father's artwork in it. I am so proud to have this for myself and my three sons to treasure always. This fine publication will remain on my bookshelf to be enjoyed by many over the years to come.

With warm regards,
—**Jennifer Virgil Gurchinoff**

Heya Peter,

The copies of *illustrators* arrived today. I'm utterly gob smacked. It's beautiful. I can't wait to see the illustrator Terry Oakes, and then the work of Les Edwards. You have done me so proud!
—**Johnny Mains**

Dear Peter,

Absolutely delighted with what you did! Could not have been better. Loved the final selection of art and the double-page spreads, two of my favourite works.
—**Anita Virgil**

We are pleased to have your views about *illustrators*, so please write to the editor, Peter Richardson, at Illustrators. The Book Palace. Jubilee House. Bedwardine Road. Crystal Palace. LONDON. SE19 3AP, or email him at *p-r@dircon.co.uk*